CONFEDERATE WOMEN OF ARKANSAS

MEMORIAL REMINISCENCES

Confederate Women of Arkansas

in the
Civil War

MEMORIAL REMINISCENCES

————————ᵈᵍᵗᵍᵈ————————

Originally published in 1907 by The United Confederate
Veterans of Arkansas

Revised, and New Material Added

with an Introduction by

Michael B. Dougan
Professor of History,
Arkansas State University

————————ᵈᵍᵗᵍᵈ————————

m & m Press
Fayetteville, Arkansas

Table of Contents

INTRODUCTION

Michael B. Dougan
Professor of History,
Arkansas State University

"Hurrah for the ladies! They are the soul of the war," an Alabama soldier mused.[1] And Arkansas observers agreed. "The Federals here say the Southern women here are the most industrious and remarkable women they have ever met with, that they keep their husbands and sons comfortably clad in the army and themselves and children neatly dressed in homespun and seem afraid of no one," wrote Professor Robert Mecklin from Fayetteville.[2] For balance, however, one must consider the comment of Junius Henri Browne, a much traveled war correspondent for the New York Tribune. Browne accompanied General Samuel Curtis' Union army into northwest Arkansas in the spring of 1862. His description of Ozark mountain women has remained classic:

> The women were only such in name; their sex, in the absence of physiological demonstration, requiring to be taken on faith. Tall, meagre, sallow, with hard features and large bones, they would have appeared masculine if

---

1. Quoted in Bell Irvin Wiley, *Confederate Women* (Westport, Conn., 1975), 140.

2. W. J. Lemke, ed., *The Mecklin Letters Written in 1863-64 at Mt. Comfort by Robert W. Mecklin* (Fayetteville, 1955), 29.

they had not been too attenuated to suggest the possibility of health or strength. They drank whisky and smoked as freely as men; often chewed tobacco, and went about swearing in discordant tones, and expectorating skillfully, and were as hideous as any Tophetian trollops that the most depraved mind could imagine.[3]

These disparate observations reflect the varieties of Arkansas women present in 1861. Although Arkansas was home to some wealthy planters' wives accustomed to being waited on by a staff of servants, the majority of Arkansas women were farm wives practicing domestic economy through food preservation, quilting, sewing, and managing vegetable and herb gardens. Frontier women smoked their pipes and drank their homemade whiskey in a world equally remote from that of both the planters and the better class of farmers. Finally, in Arkansas' few towns, the wives of merchants, shopkeepers, artisans, and workers could be found. All were affected by the great American Civil War.

In early 1861 some women worked actively to foster a war spirit. Henry M. Stanley recalled, "Even women and children cried for war. If every man did not hasten to the battle, they vowed they would themselves rush out and meet the Yankee vandals. In

---

3. Junius Henri Browne, *Four Years in Secessia: Adventures Within and Beyond the Union Lines.*(Hartford, Chicago, and London, 1865), 114.

a land where women are worshipped by the men, such language made them war-mad."[4] For many women, this fierceness coincided with an idealized vision of warfare in which women would be completely on the sidelines, innocently unaffected and perpetually respected.

Equipping troops for the war occupied many women during the spring and summer of 1861. Arkansas had a few sewing machines, and ladies in Little Rock, Camden and other towns assembled in public buildings, working frantically to send at least a few companies off to battle in proper uniforms. The ladies who gathered at Little Rock's Theatre Hall turned out 75 pairs of pants and 200 jackets a day.[5] Two of the most sartorially resplendent companies were the Camden City Guards, with "gray satinnet pants and roundabout, trimmed with red flannel stripe down the pants, coats striped shoulder cuffs with the same, leather belts," and the Camden Knights with "gray coat, roundabout, black cap, black pants, and leather belts."[6] In the rural areas companies with names like the Muddy Bayou Heroes or Arkansas Canebreakers went to war in homespun. None expected more than a summer outing, and

---

4. Dorothy Stanley, ed., *The Autobiography of Sir Henry Morton Stanley* (Boston and New York, 1937), 164-165.

5. Little Rock, *Arkansas Gazette*, May 4, 1861.

6. Michael B. Dougan, *Confederate Arkansas: The People and Policies of a Frontier State in Wartime* (University, Ala., 1976), 70.

with the onset of fall and winter, providing the soldiers with winter clothing became a matter of great concern.

During the war women served in many capacities. Nursing opportunities abounded, and soldiers remained in constant need of socks and other items of clothing. In the towns Ladies Aid societies existed, but less than one year into the war the Little Rock circle was "very poorly attended."[7] Dr. J.N. Bragg, a devoted Confederate who became increasingly caustic as the war went on, noted that assistance declined as the need grew, leaving the dead and dying with "no friendly hand to do the last kindly offices, nor no friendly ear to receive the dying messages to a wife or Mother. Do these 'Angels of Mercy' visit the sick, now that their presence and influence is needed, more than at any other time! *Not a bit of it*!"[8] "But," the good doctor observed from Little Rock, "if you will stand on a corner any fine evening, you can see the dear creatures riding on horseback, in perfect shoals, each one escorted by a man and eighteen mittens, carrying and thinking as much about the sick soldiers, as if they were so many sheep."[9] When actual danger threatened some of these women fled to Texas, and, if sufficiently supplied with

---

7. Little Rock, *Daily State Journal*, December 13, 1861.

8. Mrs. T. J. Gaughan, ed., *Letters of a Confederate Surgeon, 1861-1865* (Camden, Ark., 1960), 120-121.

9. *Ibid*.

money, lived "lives of perfect ease and indolence."[10]

Back home in Arkansas, the arrival of armies and the rise of guerilla war worked terrible hardships. Vance Randolph interviewed one woman who told him she and her sister "made two craps 'ith a yoke o' cowcritters" because all the men had fled into the bush. "Two o' my cousins," she recalled, "did git kilt right in front of our house. I was a-feedin' 'em, an' they was shot down as they run for th' horses. Th' Yankees they jest laughed an' left 'em a-layin' thar in th' road, so me an' Sis had t' dig graves an' bury 'em. Hit shore was turrible, them days."[11]

Some Arkansas women got caught up directly in the war. Fannie Hill Parley, a student at Mary Sharpe College, was at home with her family on their plantation near Cotton Plant when the Battle of Cache River erupted. She mounted her pony and took part with the Confederates in an ill-fated assault. A. C. Marshall, a Union veteran, later recalled she would have seen more fighting had she stayed at home. Fannie was "a lively girl and zealous in support of the Southern cause, one that the Union soldiers christened in a playful manner, 'The Little Rebel.' "[12] Near Helena, another became a bush-

---

10. Dougan, *Confederate Arkansas*, 114.

11. Vance Randolph, *The Ozarks—An American Survival of Primitive Society* (New York, 1931), 19-21.

12. Mrs. Dale McGregor, "The Battle of Cotton Plant," *Rivers and Roads and Points in Between*, I (Spring 1973), 9-14. The article includes a photograph of Fannie taken after her marriage.

whacker, sported a bowie knife, allegedly killed seven men, and was reported to be "on intimate terms with thieves and desperadoes on both sides."[13] One Texas soldier reported demoralization of another kind in a letter to his wife, "As we came along, I can say there is but verry few vertious ones along the road we travailed," and went on to describe encounters between the soldiers and women, adding, "Ile leave a little for you to gess at for fear some boddy sees this."[14] In short, in the ranks of Arkansas women all sorts of experiences could be recorded.

Farm women bore the brunt of the home struggle, and the collapse of their morale helped bring down the Confederate cause. Desperate letters reaching camp from home describing starvation and deprivation prompted desertions. One soldier wrote his wife, "Susan, it's enough to kill any man that thinks any thing of his family to stay away from them so long for my family is all that I can study about night or day."[15] There were women who resisted the opportunity to unburden themselves on their absent husbands. One husband, thanking his wife for her letters, observed, "Instead of making one homesick they cheer one up and make one contented and happy. I

---

13. Charles E. Nash, *Bottom Rail on Top, or Thirty Years Ago* (Little Rock, 1895), 11.

14. Robert W. Glover, "The War Letters of a Texas Conscript in Arkansas," *Arkansas Historical Quarterly*, XX (Winter 1961), 364.

15. J.T. Knight to Susan Knight, October 19, 1862. Tennessee Department of Archives and History.

think of you and the children every day, but I would
rather die and never see you anymore than to whine
around and disgrace us all. The army is a great place
to develop character."[16]

Nevertheless, war weariness set in. Dr. Bragg reported that trading with the enemy had reached even
remote Bradley County in the southern part of the
state, with the result that "the people, even to the
women, are demoralized."[17] Near the war's end, one
Helena area woman recorded in her diary, "This is a
fast day by Jeff Davis's appointment. None of us
have regarded it though. The prayers and fastings of
one or two will avail us nothing."[18]

After the war's end, women reverted to their tra-
ditional roles, and little was said about their wartime
experiences. Indeed, very little appeared in the press
about any Arkansas experiences until the publication
of the Battles and Leaders series in *Century* magazine
in the 1880s and the federal government's publication
of its official records. By the turn of the century,
however, memoirs and histories became popular, and
with the passage of each veteran into the great beyond, the whole nation was immersed in a wave of
nostalgia. Veterans organizations arose, monuments
became all the rage, and the nation gathered into its

---

16. E.P. Becton to Mrs. Becton, March 27, 1863. Becton Papers, University of Texas.

17. Gaughan, *Confederate Surgeon*, 246-247.

18. Dougan, *Confederate Arkansas*, 114.

collective consciousness for one last look at a vanished age.

The United Daughters of the Confederacy (U.D.C.) was first organized in Nashville, Tennessee, in 1890. The first Arkansas meeting occurred in Hope in 1896, and by 1930 the society had fifty chapters with 3,000 members. Dedicated to looking after the living veterans and their children, marking graves, seeing to the proper identification of the road Jefferson Davis surveyed between Dardanelle and Fort Smith, and, as one older state history put it, "teaching truths of Southern history," the U.D.C. was one of three Southern patriotic groups, the others being the United Confederate Veterans (U.C.V.) and the United Sons of Confederate Veterans (U.S.C.V.)[19]

These three organizations seem to have differed on various matters, including the erection of two monuments to the Confederacy placed on the grounds of the new state capitol.

At the beginning of the twentieth century the major promotion underway in Arkansas was the building of a new state capitol. The old state house had long been too small, was so poorly kept up that a portion of ceiling collapsed on the state senate, and failed to project the image sought by the state's business leaders. Governor Jeff Davis, however, fought the project during his three terms, and the state capitol scandal rocked Arkansas for nearly twenty years.

---

19. David Y. Thomas, ed., *Arkansas and Its People*, II (New York, 1930), 592.

The capitol was not even half finished when the monument enthusiasm hit Arkansas.[20]

The first proposed monument was to honor the Confederate dead. Fundraising efforts were begun by the Daughters and seconded by the Arkansas Gazette. Their $5,000 was then matched by the Arkansas legislature which passed Act 83 in 1903. A committee that included five Daughters chose a design submitted by F. W. Ruckstuhl. Entitled by the Arkansas Gazette as "The Defense of the Flag," Ruckstuhl's statue quietly became the "Monument to Confederate Soldiers." "I tried to show you a typical Arkansas soldier, who standing in the midst of a howling battle and general ruin and having the staff of his people's flag shot off, picks it up and holds that flag aloft at any price and sacrifice," he explained. Ruckstuhl, who did not attend the dedication, argued that bronze would age better than marble in Arkansas and noted, "In spite of the low price paid for the monument, I have tried to do my duty to the state of Arkansas."[21]

Rain caused the dedication to be delayed until June 3, 1905, which, not coincidentally, was Jefferson Davis' birthday. Over 3,000 persons attended, and the impressive ceremonies included the return by the U.S. War Department of captured Confederate flags. Roy D. Campbell, the sponsor of Act 83, gave

---

20. John A. Treon, "Politics and Concrete: The Building of the Arkansas State Capitol, 1899-1917," *Arkansas Historical Quarterly*, XXXI (Summer 1972), 99-133.

21. Little Rock, *Arkansas Gazette*, June 4, 1905, Sec. 1, p. 3.

full credit to the Daughters' lobbying efforts. Governor Jeff Davis, although a bitter opponent of the new capitol, gave the main address, dwelling on the sufferings of Jefferson Davis, and using the occasion to denounce those holding the "progressive" idea that the defeat of secession had been in the nation's best interest. "I think you old veterans were right when you fought," he announced, "that you are right now, that you have never been wrong."[22] Arkansas' quintessential demagogue the same year got into a heated verbal battle when he used his introduction of President Theodore Roosevelt to defend lynchings as sound public policy.[23]

Following Davis came Senator James H. Berry, himself a veteran (unlike Davis) and the owner of only one leg, having lost the other at the Battle of Corinth. Berry, who would be unseated by Davis from the Senate in 1906, presented the flags to Mrs. L.C. Hall of Darndanelle, who added to the day's oratory. Colonel Asa S. Morgan of Camden made the concluding remarks.[24]

Apparently, since the women had done most of the work in getting this first monument erected, the men decided to return the favor. The author of a tribute to Southern women was one Dr. G. H. Tich-

---

22. *Ibid.*

23. Raymond Arsenault, *The Wild Ass of the Ozarks: Jeff Davis and the Social Bases of Southern Politics* (Philadelphia, 1984), 210-213.

24. Little Rock, *Arkansas Gazette*, June 4, 1905, Sec. 1, p. 3.

nor of New Orleans, who launched the monument movement at the 1896 convention of the the United Confederate Veterans but made little headway. The Daughters rejected the idea in 1902, and the project languished until Gen. C. Irvine Walker of South Carolina embraced the cause. In 1910, Miss Belle Kinney of Nashville, Tennessee, agreed to design a basic monument which supporters hoped to place in every Southern state. However, the Daughters found fault with her design, even though her statue of Gen. Joseph E. Johnston at Dalton, Georgia, had been favorably received. Male supporters of the project were disappointed. "So much for the efforts of the U.D.C.," the monument's historian, Charles Coffin, observed disparagingly.[25]

Initiative then shifted back to the men. At the 1906 Arkansas U.C.V. meeting at Fort Smith, Rev. J.M. Lucey, the well-known Catholic priest from Pine Bluff, rounded up support and got a committee established to promote an Arkansas statue. Father Lucey put together a blue-ribbon group consisting of Senator Berry, Ex-Governor Dan Jones, Colonel V.Y. Cook of Batesville, and Charles Coffin. Their money-making scheme was the publication of *Confederate Women of Arkansas, 1861-1865*. This "little book," as Coffin called it, was "historically and otherwise interesting, but it was rather slow of sale," yielding the committee a net profit of something over $400.[26]

---

25. *Ibid.*, May 2, 1913, p. 1.

26. *Ibid.*

This seed money had its uses, however, and the group went to the legislature in 1911 and secured $10,000 to complete the work. Selecting a statue rent the men asunder. Half the members wanted the Kinney design; the other half rejected it. To break the tie, the committee was enlarged. The Kinney design was finally rejected, as were other suggestions, and J. Otto Schweizer's proposal, which Coffin called "the next best to the Kinney design," was chosen.[27] Curiously, nowhere in the newspaper accounts of the dedication was the sculptor's name ever given.

This statue was placed in the southeast corner of the capitol. According to Governor J.M. Futrell at the dedication, the statue represented a family scene. A son, "a type of manhood approximating perfection," is leaving for the war, his father and elder brother already having perished in the conflict. A daughter cries while the eight-year-old son plays on a toy drum. The central figure, the mother, gives her blessing to the sacrifice. "Was there ever greater sacrifice and devotion or sublimer exhibition of patriotism?" Futrell asked, "Never, never."[28] There were no addresses by women, but Josie Frazee Cappleman, the poet laureate of the Trans-Mississippi Department of the U.C.V., read "Confederate Womanhood." As a summary of the social ideas of conservative Southern women and the creative force behind both the book and the monument, it deserves to be quoted in full:

---

27. *Ibid.*

28. *Ibid.*

Greetings, Women of the Sixties,
    Greetings Men, that War withstood;
For this day we come to honor
    Our Southern Womanhood.
She, who shared the hazards, hardships
    With our heroes, side by side;
She, the mother, wife and daughter
    Of those who fought and died.

She, the sad-eyed Southern Mother —
    All too proud to shed a tear;
Yet, who braved War's blackest terrors
    Without falter, fall or fear.
I can see her watching, waiting
    For the Boy that never came.
Who is lying, somewhere, mangled
    In a grave without a name.

And when Lee said: "Cease Firing,"
    And th' Southland's hopes lay dead,
She waged the fiercer battle —
    The battle, then for bread.
The soft, white hands of culture
    By toil were hardened then,
While her words of cheer and comfort
    Revived disheartened men.

Men, whose lives were bruised and broken
    'Mid desolation's reign.
Who had lost their all in anguish,
    And whose brother-man lay slain

On fields, once full and fragrant
    With the season's richest mead;
Where smoke and wreck and ruins
    Marked a foeman's direful deed.

It was she who took up the burden,
    In this shattered Land of Song,
Where the homes were heaps of ashes
    And only hearts left strong.
Aye; these women, gently nurtured,
    Sweet-tuned to every grace,
Worked hand in hand with husbands —
    Helped the ruined home replace.

So, today, we come to honor
    The sacrificial deeds.
Of the Women of the Sixties,
    Who served their Country's needs.
'Tis for you, who still are spared us,
    As for those, long passed away: —
"To the South's heroic women,
    From the Veterans of the Gray."

Brave Soldiers of the Sixties,
    This day a debt is paid
Which your chivalry demanded,
    Ere dust to dust was laid.
All honor to these Veterans,
    As gallant now as then;
The Knighthood of the Nations,
    The noblest of men!

Sweet Women of the Sixties,

Brave hearts beneath the gray,
All love, all joy, all honor,
Be yours, this gala day!
May these truths, in bronze and marble,
Be a lesson, grand and good,
For the youth of coming ages,
Of true Southern Womanhood.[29]

At the unveiling, the band played "Just Before the Battle, Mother," a favorite Civil War song but one of Yankee origins. In contrast to the strident Southern nationalism expressed by Jeff Davis in 1905, veterans in blue and gray were seated side by side.[30]

Governor J. N. Futrell used the occasion to observe that the ideals of a country could be found engraved in its memorial monuments. The two statues on the capitol grounds reflect an idealization popular in the early twentieth century, not the reality of the grim and vicious war fought in Arkansas. Today, with World Wars I and II, Korea and Vietnam as part of our experience, these monuments appear quaint and charming, bereft of the strong emotive power they once possessed. Their idealized world is, surprisingly, not always echoed in this little book.

---

29. *Ibid*.

30. Willard A. and Porter W. Heaps, *The Singing Sixties; The Spirit of Civil War Days Drawn from the Music of the Times* (Norman, 1960), 133. George F. Root was the composer; but the song was popular on both sides.

Defying the conventions of heroic gentility, some women kept alive in their minds the core truth of what the Civil War had actually been. Their stories provide a redeeming touch of realism and warrant a modern generation of readers to look again at the roles women played in our great American tragedy.

Publishers Note

In making the decision to completely reset this book instead of doing a photographic reproduction of the original, the publisher decided to omit some of the "filler material" which appeared in the original, mostly newpaper anecdotes. Also, some spelling corrections were made and some stylistic changes, such as capitalization. The stories themselves were not altered. Those who have seen the original volume will note that we have included an Index with this edition.

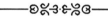

Preface to 1907 Edition

The State Annual Reunion of the Arkansas United Confederate Veterans, held at Fort Smith, October 17-19, 1906 appointed, through the commander, Gen. N. T. Roberts, a committee of five veterans, J. H. Berry, V. Y. Cook, Charles Coffin, Dan W. Jones and J. M. Lucey, to arrange for the cooperation of the United Confederate Veterans of Arkansas and Sons of Veterans with the general committee of the United Confederates of the South for the erection of at least one monument in each of the Southern States to commemorate the heroism of the Southern women in the Civil War period.

STARTED FIVE YEARS AGO

This monument movement came into prominence five years ago, when the fact began to dawn upon the minds of the old veterans and sons of veterans that the women of the South had borne a very conspicuous part in the glorious achievements of the Southern soldiery, so much so that had it not been for their superb nobility of character in cheerfully bidding what was often a last farewell to their loved ones and in working away the beauty and tenderness of Southern rearing in country and town to support their lonely families, the war could not have been sustained for any considerable length of time. But when this fact did finally dawn upon the minds of the old veterans, they resolved to attest their appreciation of the greatness of the Southern women, who excelled the historic Roman matron and Spartan mother, by gathering and publishing the reminiscences of the work of the women of the South in the Civil war period and by erecting at least one monument in each Southern State to commemorate their heroism.

Gen. C. Irvine Walker, Charleston, S. C., commander of the U. C. V. Department of the Army of Northern Virginia, was made chairman at the Louisville reunion, three years ago, of the general committee. This committee has succeeded in gathering and publishing in newspaper supplements the chronicles of the work of Southern women in several Southern States, notably South Carolina, Virginia and Tennessee. This work will be pushed to completion in the remaining States of the South.

Gen. Walker's committee have also accomplished considerable work on the question of a monument to Southern women. It has been decided that the monument be of bronze. Designs were called for last year and, at the meeting of the committee after the adjournment of the Richmond reunion of the present year a selection of a design was made. The committee are now selecting the artist who is to carry out their wishes and supervise the casting of the monuments. Within a short time the artist will be selected and the next step will be to estimate the cost of each monument for a State and to apportion it. The veterans and sons of veterans of each State will be asked to share State by State, in the expense incurred. It is impossible just now to estimate exactly what each State will have to pay as a pro rata for a monument. Perhaps five thousand dollars is approximate. Each monument will be an original under this plan and the uniformity throughout the South will be a striking feature. Everywhere will be seen that face and figure of Southern beauty and power, looking down with inspiring love and tenderness upon the rising generations of the Southland.

ARKANSAS COMMITTEE

Our Arkansas committee met in Little Rock last winter and organized for work along these lines. It was discovered that quite a large number of papers written by Southern ladies of the State and full of interesting reminiscenses were in the hands of J. Kellogg, Little Rock, as the result of a previous effort in this direction. At the above meeting J. M. Lucey was made chairman and J. Kellogg was made honorary member of the board and elected secretary. The chairman was empowered to collect all accessible papers and to solicit new ones from the ladies of the State; all of which were to be carefully supervised by him and then published in a pamphlet form, rather than a newspaper supplement. It was, however, decided to publish the papers first in the Sunday edition of the Arkansas Gazette and after submission to their authors to print them in a pamphlet of an edition of 3,000 copies.

The Memorial Committee were able to report to the State Reunion U. C. V., held October 4-5, this year, at Hot Springs, Ark., that the work of going over the old papers and collecting new ones was practically completed. All of the old papers, with possibly two or three exceptions, have appeared in the Sunday edition of the Arkansas Gazette. None of the new series of papers have been given to the Gazette, as it was only recently that the final copy of the old series was used, and it is thought best to get out the pamphlet without further delay. The report of the Memorial Committee was unanimously approved by the Reunion, and the Committee was made a permanent one, and authorized to publish three thousand copies of the pamphlet and to arrange a plan to canvass the principal cities of the State to raise five thousand dollars for the monument to the Confederate Women of Arkansas of the Civil War period.

This volume is, therefore, published under the auspices of the United Confederate Veterans of Arkansas, as a tribute to the women of the South, and a slight acknowledgement of their many sucessful efforts to glorify the Confederate soldier. No effort has been made to give these papers a literary dress. They are given in the simple language and style in which they were orginally written. They will become a most desirable addition to the material that will some day be used to make up a satisfactory history of the mighty struggle of the North and South over forty years ago, as each paper contains some particular incident of historic value.

To render our volume more complete and perhaps more attractive, several selections have been inserted which refer to subjects dear to every Confederate heart; History of the Origin of the U. C. V., of the U. S. C. V., and of the Daughters; of the Confederate Uniform and Flag of the Confederate Museum and the Memorial Association, and similar things. War songs and poems which have become historic are given, and finally anecdotes of camp life are presented not merely to relieve the heavier reading but to bring forward a feature of Confederate life that historians covet.

Few Confederate Veterans will read these pages with dry eyes. They will read of Sterling Price's body guard of eighty men appearing on the streets of Camden from their Missouri raid with sockless feet and almost frozen when the Southern ladies gave every man of them a pair of socks and some of them shoes and then worked day and night, Sunday and week-day, to make up the deficit for the boxes they were sending to their own loved ones on distant battlefields. They will read of tenderly raised Southern women working in the fields alone with negro servants to raise a simple crop, that was to be carried off by Federal raiders.

The women who wove and spun the clothing of the Southern soldier and their own, who risked their lives in bearing important dispatches to Confederate generals, who spent days and nights at the cot of the soldier in the hospital and who have cared for the graves of the Confederate dead even to the extent of erecting countless memorial monuments and leaving their own heroism to be unnoticed, if not unknown, deserve to be commemorated in the grandest records and finest monument that man's genius can devise. The old Confederate veterans of Arkansas would otherwise indeed be ungrateful to the noble women who stood by the Southern cause in war and, when all was lost but honor, received the broken-down father, husband and brother, without a tear or anything but comforting words and cheerful smiles.

> J. M. LUCEY, Chairman,
> DAN W. JONES,
> CHARLES COFFIN,
> V. Y. COOK,
> J. H. BERRY,
> J. KELLOGG, Secretary.

Committee of the Arkansas Division, U. C. V., on Memorial to the Women of the Confederacy.

REMINISCENCES OF THE WAR BETWEEN THE STATES

By Mrs. Eugene R. Goodwin, of Augusta

In April of 1861, there was the wildest excitement in Augusta, Ark., when the first company of mounted rifles was being formed. Manly hearts burning to go to the defence of their country, and yet yearning anxiously for the loved and defenceless ones they must leave behind them. Wives, mothers, sisters, and sweethearts struggling bravely to conceal their own bitter heartaches, that they might strengthen and cheer their dear ones, for the hard duties that lay before them. But there was neither time, nor opportunity for any sentimental indulgence of any of these feelings: the most strenuous activity was imperative.

Women must be taught the use of fire-arms that they might be able to defend themselves and their homes. Their first awkward efforts proved the occasion of much grim mirth, while some soon became good marksmen.

There was no government to supply clothing for the soldiers, so the merchants furnished material, and women gathered in numbers to cut and make the grey uniforms and knitting socks became the pastime and rest-work of busy fingers in all the odd minutes.

But as we look back, all this seems but pleasure compared with what followed. Orders soon came for "all volunteers to report in Little Rock." Now, the romance is all gone, and the fearful realities are upon us. We must make them a flag, and it must be presented in

1

due form. In the presence of an immense crowd, our gallant boys clothed in their grey uniforms and mounted on their war steeds were reined up in line before a stand from which a frail girl, trembling with emotion, after an address full of martial fervor, patriotism and confidence in the courage and heroism of the brave hearts before her, handed the flag to the standard bearer.

Upon receiving it, he made a short chivalric reply and every hat went up and every throat hurrahed for "the courage of our women and the sacredness of our Cause." Then galloping from this portentous scene, all were soon engaged in preparations for the final parting on the morrow.

As the boat upon which the troops were to embark steamed up to the wharf, friends and relatives crowded around our heroes and who shall tell of the anguish that wrung those hearts in that last parting? The picture of that boat, as she rounded the bend in the river, the boys' caps and handkerchiefs waving, some singing and others shouting, every attitude giving expresssion to the depth of their emotion, still stands out in bold relief upon memory's tablet and refuses to be effaced by the occurences of more than forty years.

I shall not open the pages of memory that tell of the bitterness that followed. There were no mails to bring tidings from the loved ones, and harrowing rumors were continually reaching us of their sufferings and privations, so that we were forced in many ways to feel that the "horrors of war" were upon us.

Tho' some distance from the seat of war, we were often subjected to visits from small bodies of troops, sent on some mission by one or other of the contending armies.

The first rumor of the *enemy's* coming struck terror into every heart. We feared everything, but escaped, this time, with only the loss of any and everything they could eat, wear or carry off.

On one occasion, when our Capt. Rutherford and his men had been giving the enemy considerable trouble, they sent a small body of troops to surprise and capture them. Coming up on the opposite bank of White River and finding no means of crossing over into the town, a number of the most reckless and daring among them doffed every article of clothing, swam the river and with shameless effrontery, paraded our streets in an absolutely nude state. Instantly every door and blind was closely shut; curtains drawn; and the whole town was as still as death.

A negro man was hastily despatched to warn them not to approach too near any dwelling for the women of that town were well armed and well drilled in the use of firearms. The faithful negro adding in his own persuasive way "And I tell you gemmans, if you step your foot in one of dem yards, you won't neber hab no more use for cloes."

They gave full credit to this kindly hint and at once recrossed the river and we heard of them no more, and our hearts went up in a hymn of praise to our God for this special deliverance.

Another trying time was when Curtis's army came thro' our town. My mother still had with her the negro man mentioned above (her carriage driver in slave times) to whom—by the way, let me just here pay a well-deserved tribute. During all the years of the war, he seemed to feel that he was duty bound to work for and protect his mistress and her family. He regularly brought to her all his earnings; and was as loyal in every way as the truest and noblest son, or brother could have been. He was at once sent to the General's headquarters for "a guard" and with a request that he permit some worthy officer to board with us during his stay in our town. He sent us quite a polished, pleasant gentleman, Capt. of an Indiana Company.

This proved a boon to us, for he not only treated us beautifully, but saw that we and all we had, were carefully protected from depreciations and indignities to which others were subjected. When the command moved on and left our town, there was a rumor that they had found us to be such fire-eating rebels that stragglers had been ordered to remain behind and burn the town that night. We had no men, but the women held a council and we decided to form ourselves into a police force and patrol the town all night. This we did; walking our several beats as faithfully, if not as fearlessly, as any city police. Whether or not the rumor had been baseless, we never knew, but our town was not burned.

Once the dreaded cry "The Federals are coming" caught a wounded confederate soldier "laying up for repairs" in my mother's home. What to do we knew not. There was no chance to get him out of town. We knew there were some in town who would inform on us; then, of course, would follow a thorough search of our home and premises. So, after a hurried consultation my pale face and wasted form (being just out of a severe spell of sickness) suggested a way out of our dilemma. Earnestly praying God's blessings on our plan, we decided to arrange one room as for a very sick person. We arranged a table filled with medicines and other sick room paraphernalia; stationed a nurse; darkened the room; and placed the wounded soldier between the mattress and feather bed; then put me to bed, arranging the feathers to conceal the unnatural bump in that bed.

We tried to keep the whole house in a hush to awe them into not making the search if possible but they were not so easily turned aside. They bluntly stated "They had orders to search this house and they intended to search it." We could not even prevail upon them to spare the sick room, tho' we entreated with tears (which were not in our plans.) They filed in, peered everywhere; even under the patient's bed and punched, with their bayonets, every suspicious looking object, then quietly left the room; leaving me trembling with fear—my fears being mischievously aggravated by hearing much bemuffled whispers "You are smothering me to death" and many like remarks, coming from the hiding place of our wounded Reb, ere my mother considered it safe to let him out.

But by God's blessing on our efforts, one more soldier was spared to fight to the end of the war and is now a wealthy and prominent citizen of Shreveport, Louisiana.

Just one more incident and I will close. When the Fitzhugh fight occurred the Yankees were still trying to capture or wipe out Capt. Rutherford's command. Having failed in all previous attempts, they sent a gunboat up from Helena with a force of about four hundred fighting men aboard. They landed at Augusta, sent out their troops, leaving the crew and a few officers in charge of the boat. These officers entertained themselves during the day by calling on young ladies. Being in use as a female academy at that time, our house was especially attractive to them. They were very courteous and polite; "hoped we would pardon them, but they were very anxious to make the acquaintance of some of the Southern girls." We didn't dare repulse them but discouraged their attentions by our manners and the assurance that we felt only bitterness towards their cause and their armies. They met all this with the most patient, forbearing politeness, telling us those feelings were very natural now, but after a while we would feel differently. This so exasperated us that when they begged for music, we told them we knew only Southern war songs, and to their request, "Then sing them for us" we selected the bitterest we knew, throwing all the spirit into them that was then almost bursting our hearts. They not only listened very kindly, but seemed really to enjoy our "rebel"songs. But soon the fight was on. We could hear the firing and we very excitedly and confidently told them: "Now you will have to go, for our men will whip or capture all your troops." They hooted at such a thought but very calmly and gallantly bade us goodbye and started for the boat, and before they reached the wharf, their men came flying in, hotly pursued (as they thought) by the victorious "rebels." And very soon their gunboat was steaming down stream. This was too good a chance, we just couldn't resist the temptation to sing, with wildest enthusiasm, "We'll hurl the Yankee crew from the land we love the best."

Now it happened our house and Academy was not two hundred yards from the river, so we were in full view, and this volume of song, triumphantly welling up from ten or fifteen young ladies was more than the defeated Yankees could stand, so they turned loose their cannon on us. But the river was narrow and the banks were very high, at that point, so their balls only cut some of the highest tree tops.

————————ට&ෳ·ෳ&ට————————

SIGEL'S RAIDERS BURN A FINE HOME
By Mrs. Homer F. Sloan, of Augusta

One of the hardest things to understand about war, especially by women, is the flagrant destruction of homes and necessaries of life. General Franz Sigel was exiled from Germany because of his advocacy of popular government. He was given a high position in the Union army in order to gratify the German soldiers who had entered the army in large numbers. Such a man should be expected to have manly and generous sentiments. The following incident of his raid near Augusta shows how brutal he was:

On a large plantation near Augusta, Ark., in 1862 was an old Southern home. There were 200 negro slaves contentedly working and the land was in a fine state of cultivation. But in the roomy comfortable old house which the blue-coats surrounded was only an old woman and her daughter.

"Don't seem to be any men 'round?" questioned an officer.

"All gone to fight the Yankees," answered the woman promptly.

Then a soldier came up to the officer, saying, "There is only a small quantity of meat in the smoke house." When questioned as to where the rest of the meat was hidden, the woman refused to tell. Threatened with the burning of her home if she did not direct them to the place of concealment, she still refused, saying that over 200 people on the place were depending upon her for food.

"'But,' said the officer, "what will you do? You can save your house by giving up the meat.

"No." she replied, "I cannot let my people starve; as for the house, there are plenty of logs in the woods to build another one."

A soldier led around a beautiful horse and at once the girl ran to it and caught the bridle, begging them not to take her pet. Fine old furniture was broken and thrown from the windows and doors; great feather beds and pillows were carried into the yard and ripped open with knives. But the woman sat under a tree placidly knitting—deaf alike to threats and destruction.

"What are you knitting?" inquired one.

"Socks for the Confederate soldiers."

"How many pairs have you made?"

"So many that I can rib them, turn the heel and toe them off in the dark."

"How many have you on hand?"

"Not a pair; sent them away yesterday."

The negroes denied knowing anything about where the meat was hidden, the girl continued pleading to keep her horse, the old woman knitted in silence. Finally the order to start the fire was given. Then the officer said each of them might have one thing saved for them out of the house. The mother said to give her her sewing machine, and it was set near her; the girl chose her piano and it was brought out; then the torch did the work. The girl was allowed to lead her horse as she went to stand beside ber mother. Thus the enemy left them to see the destruction of their home, the old woman knitting, knitting, the young woman standing quiet, one arm thrown over her horse's neck—a picture of war's cruelty, and illustration of woman's sacrifice and fortitude.

———————————ᴅ§ᴣ·ᴇ·§ᴁ———————————

PERSONAL RECOLLECTIONS OF 1863
By Mrs. Emily S. Reed, of Batesville

After a lapse of more than forty years, events that happened so long ago must have been of a very startling nature to retain still a vivid place in memory. It has been said, that there are three things that leave ineffaceable impressions, excessive joy, grief and fright; and the last certainly did for awhile prevail over all other feelings on the occasion I now recall.

The winter of eighteen hundred and sixty-three was unusually severe at Batesville, Ark., and people were in no condition to face the hardships and privations that steadily grew worse, as first one army and then the other held this country. They consumed what little was raised on the farms by women and small boys, (all able-bodied men being in the army), and the question of daily rations for the family was growing to be a very serious one. I have known girls to ride horseback ten and often twenty miles to get a peck of meal and a few pounds of flour, and they considered themselves lucky indeed to find a little dried fruit. Early in February, I forget the exact date, the weather grew much colder, and ended in a heavy snow, which added greatly to the discomfort already prevailing.

GERMAN FEDERAL RAIDERS SUDDENLY APPEAR

One of my brothers was at home sick in bed. One evening, mother, my younger brothers and myself were in the sitting room with him, when mother asked me to go out in the dining room and get a glass of water to mix some medicine. To reach the dining room, I had to go down two steps on the back porch on which both it and the kitchen opened. I went through the door of the former, got the glass and water, and turned to go back when happening to glance toward the window, I saw what literally paralyzed me with fright, and instant death seemed before me, for there at the window were crowded a lot of hideous, grinning "feds," jabbering in Dutch and pointing at me. I was simply scared silly, but had sense enough to run for my life, and burst into the sitting room white as a ghost, with eyes so full of horror, that mother came flying to me, saying, "Em, what's the matter?" Just as I gasped out. "Mother, the yard is full of 'feds'!" in they poured, back door and front door, crowding and jabbering some orders in Dutch, which, of course, none of us understood, at which they were getting very angry with us, until one officer the first American we had seen, pushed his way in and ordered mother to get supper for fifty men. She calmly (while I wondered how she could talk at all), replied, that there wasn't enough in the whole neighborhood to feed that many. He made an angry reply and told his men to help themselves, which they lost no time in doing.

DRIED APPLES BUSTING "FEDS"

First, they tied their horses all over the yard to a lot of young fruit trees, then broke open the store room, etc., soon demolishing what was on hand. I remember noticing (after I had gotten partly over my scare) a few big Dutch fellows ravenously "getting away" with a bag of dried apples, which had quite recently been sent to mother from the country, and for which she had exchanged salt, and the sight recalled a conversation I once heard between two little boys on the dried apple question. One boy had a pocket full of this fruit and the other wanted " a divide," which being refused, he said, "My ma says dried apples raw will swell up and bust you!" which I fervently hoped might be realized in the present instance.

WARING'S COMMAND OF RAIDERS

They took possession of anything they saw, and carried things their own way, we meanwhile being all crowded together in the sitting room, glad to know we were still alive. At twelve o'clock, when Colonel Waring and staff arrived, he took our parlor for headquarters, and ordered those Dutch around, like so many dogs, — "begging a dog's pardon!" After his arrival matters did not look so "skeery," for this officer, though a "Fed," was a gentleman in manner, and was very profuse in his apologies to mother, — said "she should be amply remunerated for any and all damages she had sustained, to which he would attend personally, as he was now in command of this section," (which 'tis needless to say was all "bosh,") as his stay was brief, though long enough to leave a heavy mark wherever that Dutch gang raided Batesville that night. Among other things, I think, they found a large quantity of sugar in the basement of the court house, belonging to Geo. Case, which they wantonly destroyed.

That was truly a night of terror in Batesville, and even at this late day a sort of "chill" runs over me when I think of those *awful "Feds"* at the window, when I realized for the first time, what it meant "to be scared silly."

Towards day-break, the whole command moved swiftly north, and a few hours later, Gen. Shelby crossed the river with about three thousand men, and followed them a short distance.

It seems this command was reported to be the advance guard of a large force of Federals coming here, but was in reality about five hundred Dutch, known as "Waring's Command," on one of their notorious raids through southern Missouri and north Arkansas.

SHE KNEW HER BOYS

During the War Between the States a rumor of "battle at Seven Pines" reached a remote part of Virginia, but as yet there were no details. A mother had two sons — John and James — in the same company, and anxiety found expression in the oft repeated lament: "Poor John, I know, I know he's killed or wounded."

The husband and father at last became annoyed at the repeated mention of John to the exclusion of James, and exclaimed:

"What about James? You love him equally with John. Why don't you think of him?"

The mother replied: "My poor John! James is all right, husband, for there are seven trees there, and I know that James is behind one of them."

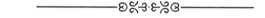

PRIVATIONS OF A SOLDIER'S WIDOW
By Mrs. M. M. Hendrix, of Big Fork

My husband Benjamin Franklin Hendrix entered the Southern army in the beginning of the war, joining Captain Edwin's company, Fourth Arkansas infantry, in June, 1861. He was killed in battle December 15, 1863, leaving me with four little children, to live the hard life of many a Confederate widow. My oldest child, George Washington, was seven years old; the next, Samuel Enoch, was five; the third was Benjamin Franklin, three years old, and the youngest, Sarah Elizabeth, was only ten months old.

I felt all these things the more because I was an adopted citizen of Arkansas. My native home was in Pickens County, South Carolina, where I was born October 17, 1832. My parents moved to Cherokee County, Ga., when I was about one year old. At the age of 12, I came with my parents to Montgomery County,

Arkansas, and September 4, 1852, married Benjamin F. Hendrix, who was the same age as myself, 22 years.

FEDERAL RAIDERS TOOK EVERYTHING

With four little ones to provide for, I found life a hard problem. Many times when night came and I lay down, I could not sleep on account of my destitute condition, and being forced to see my children suffer from cold and hunger without power or prospect of helping them. I could have managed to live fairly well, as I could work in the field and chop wood and I had some provisions laid by and the house was comfortably furnished, but Federal soldiers came and robbed me of everything, not leaving a mouthful at times for myself and little ones.

They were frequently brutal and once when I seemed slow about cooking something for them, they began cursing and pointed a gun at me, so that I was terribly frightened. But God was good to me in keeping me in a Christian spirit, and I succeeded in raising all my children. My son, G. W. Hendrix, lives at Black Springs, Ark.; Samuel E. Hendrix, lives at Ultimathule, Ark.; B. F. Hendrix lives at Maxwell, I. T., and my daughter, Sarah Elizabeth, lives at Big Fork, Ark., and is happily married to Mr. Liles.

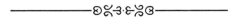

A STORY OF THE LEES

The visit of Gen. Fitzhugh Lee, says the Louisville Courier-Journal has started a story which he told on himself several years ago, and which is a good illustration of the love the Confederate soldiers bore toward Gen. Robert E. Lee. As it is well known, Gen. Fitzhugh Lee was at the head of the cavalry, and these were much envied by the infantrymen, who had to walk through the mud and dust.

After General Robert E. Lee had surrendered, Gen. Fitzhugh Lee rode away from Appomattox. While riding through a lane he met an old North Carolina soldier.

"Ho, there," cried General Lee, "where are you going?"

"I've been off on a furlough and am now going back to join Gen. Bob Lee, replied the soldier.

"You needn't go back, but can throw your gun away and return home, for Lee's surrendered."

"Lee's surrendered ?"

"That's what I said," said General Lee.

"It must have been that damned Fitz Lee, then. Rob Lee would never surrender," and the old soldier put on a look of contempt and walked on.

BRAVERY OF MISS LINNIE HUTCHINSON
By Maj. W. F. Forbes, of Brinkley

There is one sweet Southern girl, a cousin of mine, who has long since passed to her reward, of whom I feel it a duty to speak, Miss Linnie Hutchison. Her work did not pertain much to Arkansas, but she was well known to H. C. Tipton, former state treasurer, and others.

WHEN THE YANKEES TOOK MEMPHIS

The first Confederate company of Horn Lake, Miss., where we lived, was made up March 1, 1861, and we were ordered to Pensacola, Fla. When the Yankees took Memphis my uncle's fine home and farm became a regular raiding ground for them. My uncle was 75 years old and Miss Linnie quite a girl. For 24 miles from Memphis to Hernando the Federals burned everything combustible and not a cow, horse, hog or chicken was left. They were three years in this work of devastation and all this time Linnie Hutchinson was subjected to every possible insult and injury.

ROUTED FIFTY YANKS

The house was burned to the ground and the old man and young girl took up their abode in a negro cabin. Miss Linnie had practiced much with pistol and gun, as the necessity of being able to defend herself dawned upon her young mind. When the Feds would come into her yard, she stood, pistol in hand, ready for anything. One day a company of fifty entered the yard and began shooting every chicken in sight. Standing upon the cabin porch and raising her gun, she declared that she would shoot the man that fired the next shot at her chickens. They vacated the yard without further ado. She saved one old horse, old Mike, the buggy horse, but only after a fierce struggle in which several soldiers, threw her round and round as she clung to the bridle until blood gushed from her wrists.

Her only brother, James Hutchinson, was killed at the battle of Franklin, Tenn., falling with Gen. Pat Cleburne.

BRAVE, BUT JUST AND TENDER

A neighbor boy, Willie White, was a Union man. Some raiding Federals thought he was a bushwhacker and shot him thirteen times until death came to his relief. That brave Southern girl, Confederate to the core of her heart, knowing that Billie Brown was an honest man, went down on her knees to beg his life from his cruel captors.

FAITHFUL OLD NEGROES

There were twenty-five negroes on the Hutchinson plantation during the war and no white people except an old man and a weak young woman. Nothing went wrong. The negroes were faithful. They helped on all occasions to hide things and never told the Yankees. They made a living during the four years of the war for white and black. Old Aunt Sasa was a constant guard over Miss Linnie, frequently remaining up all night when danger was anticipated.

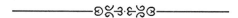

A HEROINE OF CHICKAMAUGA

During the preliminary manoeuvers which preceded the battle of Chickamauga, Manigault's brigade was in position near a small farm, the humble log cabin of which masked the poverty of the owner, but close to this was a patch of luscious sorghum cane, into which the boys found their way and commenced to forage. As they were in the midst of the cane breaking it and sucking the juicy portions, two newcomers appeared on the scene, Colonel Sawyer, of the Twenty-fourth Alabama regiment, and the owner. The colonel promptly ordered the men out, but the old woman interfered; her dress and appearance indicated how dependent she was upon that little patch for part of her support, but her heart was warm for the cause. "Colonel," she said, "that's my sorghum; I raised it, but these are my boys; let them have all they want. Pitch in boys and help yourselves."

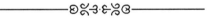

SKETCH OF MRS. LUTETIA M. HOWELLS, OF CLARKSVILLE
By her daughter, Mrs. Sallie E. Jordan, of Clarksville.

It is with the greatest reluctance that I write this sketch of my mother's experience during the Civil war. If those who have urged me so much and so often to write, knew what I have suffered in putting those sad particulars on paper, they would have said, "let them alone." Those who have undertaken to gather reminiscences of this kind have a hard task on their hands as one-thousandth part of what the women of the South suffered during the war can never be told. It is a duty, however, that the authors of these reminiscences should be aided in every possible way, so that valuable materials of history may not be lost. This is why I send my crude statements, though it is breaking my heart to do so.

At the time of the burning of my mother and aunt, my father, S. J. Howell, had gone to Texas with our servants. My brother, Captain J. B. Howell, was ordinance officer of General James F. Fagan. Our home was in a little town on the Arkansas River, called Pittsburg, about nine miles from Clarksville. The Federal officer in command of Clarksville at the time was Col. Waugh. He had never been known to do a kind act for any citizen until my mother's awful treatment happened, when he begain to act as a human being. One Federal officer called and said to me: "If my wife or mother had been treated as yours, I would live only to kill Federals and when I came to die, I would regret that I could not live longer to kill more."

The following are the main particulars: On the night of the 20th of February, 1864, five or six Federal soldiers came and demanded money of mother, saying, "I know you have it, every one knows that your husband has plenty of money." When she refused to give them money, they stripped the right foot and leg and thrust it into a bed of red hot coals lying in a large open fireplace. When they took it out they asked her if she would tell them where the money was, and when she said no, they put it back and told her they would burn her to death if she did not tell. The flesh was cooked until it fell off from the knee to the toe. They then brought in my widowed aunt Mrs. John W. Willis, who was living with my mother. They had been keeping her outside on the lawn, and had previously told her that my mother had sent her word to tell them where the money was, as they were burning her to death. She said she did not believe them and refused. They then took my mother from the fire and put my aunt in, and burned her in the same way, but not quite so severely. At last when they found they were of the material from which heroines are made and Spartan mothers reared, they released them and going to the servants quarters, they locked them in and told them if they came out before sun up, their heads would be shot off. My poor mother in some way found the linseed oil and together she and my aunt dressed their burns. Next morning the three negro women in great fear came to them and did what they could for them. Later on these women took the week's laundry and went across the hill, a quarter of a mile from the house, where there was a fine spring, to do the washing; the hill hid this house from their view. Later on one of the women started back to see if there was anything needed. When she reached the top of the hill, she saw the flames bursting out from the roof. When mother and aunt learned that the house was on fire, they in some mysterious way with those terribly burned limbs, crawled to the wood pile, where they lay and watched the destruction of a fine old Southern home (the home where brother John and I were reared). When the building was falling into ashes some Federal officers came with ambulances, to fill them with furnishings from this house. When they saw the sad plight of my loved ones, they were compelled to take them to Clarksville, where they could receive medical attention. I must say Drs. Root and Adams of Kansas, in whose charge they were placed, were exceedingly kind to them. A week after this terrible affair Capt. Abbot, commanding a U. S. transport, (but a Southern sympathizer), came down from Clarksville and sent me word, saying, that he had not the courage to bring the message in person. Capt. Abbot held the transport until I could get ready to return with him. I left my four fatherless children, (baby being quite ill), with my dear friend, Mrs. Adams, widow of ex-Governor Samuel Adams, step-mother of Capt. John D. Adams, and mother of Gen. Jas. F. Fagan. Mrs. Adams was afterwards with me in Little Rock, having been turned out of her home by Federal officers. It took the transport three days to reach Spadra Bluff, the nearest point by river to Clarksville. I was told here that mother was dying and that her limb had been amputated, all of which was almost unbearable for me, and the suffering so changed me that some of my loved ones did not recognize me. I must pass over the meeting with my mother; I can not even at this late day write of it. I staid until my mother could be moved to Spadra Bluff by ambulance, and by transport to my home in Little Rock. The news soon spread that we had arrived. The first to reach the boat was our old friend, Dr. R. L. Dodge. He dropped on his knees beside mother's bed and wept aloud. Mother did not die just at this time, but lingered two years. Poor, dear mother, how she suffered! "I forgive them for the pain and poverty they have caused me," were her words. They destroyed what they could not carry away, shooting large numbers of cattle, hogs, etc.

Maj. Newsome (a Federal), told me at Spadra, that when mother's house was on fire, he counted fourteen others burning at the same time, and he knew that orders for the fires had been sent out from headquarters.

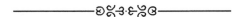

HEROIC DEEDS OF SOUTHERN WOMEN
By Mrs. K. D. Goodbar, of Charleston

Mrs. Catherine Haynes, whose home is near Charleston, Arkansas, is one of the oldest and most interesting of the few remaining women in that section who worked, suffered and endured, for the "Lost Cause."

She is living out her sunset years in the same old family homestead, which was once the scene of so much stirring adventure, and her recollections of those trying days are still fresh and unobscured, though Time is laying his hand heavily now upon her silvered locks.

Mrs. Haynes and her two daughters, Miss Lizzie and Miss Sarah Jane, are known to have buried, or assisted in burying, at least six, perhaps more of our fallen heroes, which was certainly no mean service. She has often been heard to relate the following incident:

Six men belonging to Col. McIntosh's regiment were quietly eating breakfast in one of three small cottages, built close to the Haynes' homestead. Mrs. Tobb, a Union woman, Mrs. Roberts, and Mrs. Knott, a widow, were the occupants of the houses. The men were totally unsuspicious of any danger, but were suddenly attacked by a small party, and three of them were shot down in Mrs. Roberts' yard, while the others escaped. The names of the three soldiers killed were: Perkins, Tom Jones, and Milton Hayes, all of them closely related to men widely known in this section of the State. Mrs. Tobb ran alone all the way to the Haynes' home to tell the awful news, and to get assistance in caring for the bodies. There was not a man left on the Haynes' place so Miss Lizzie and, Miss Sarah Jane accompanied Mrs. Tobb to the scene of the tragedy, determined that not one of our brave boys should lack a decent burial so long as there were tender, pitying hands to perform the last sad duties.

Nixon's graveyard was a full half-mile distant, but one of them knew of an empty grave which had been dug for the body of a Captain Bean who had been carried back home to Roseville, and buried there instead. There was one available vehicle. It was a small cart, roughly constructed, and mounted upon two old wagon wheels. To this was harnessed the only team—a brace of young steers. With Mrs. Knott driving and two of the other women walking behind to hold the lifeless bodies on the shaky cart, from which they were in imminent danger of falling, the pathetic little procession wended its way to the graveyard. With their own hands they laid the three bodies, uncoffined, in the same grave, and with an old shovel and a rusty spade, these faithful and heroic women put the clods of "earth to earth and ashes to ashes," upon the sacred dead.

Finally worn out with physical exertion and mental emotion, they turned wearily homeward. It was nearing the close of day when at last they arrived, and bright stars, just peeping out from the grey twilight, were soon to shed their cold unfeeling radiance upon the dark tragedies of human life.

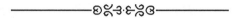

"DON'T LET THE OLD MAN BLEED ON THE BISCUITS"

Four or five members of Company H, Fifth Mississippi, while lying in the trenches around Atlanta in 1864, had a brief respite one morning from the annoying shot and shell. We had got a large lot of biscuits, and expected to have a fine time of it in enjoying the unusual banquet. But human hopes often deceive us. While we were sitting a la Turk on a blanket, pitching into the biscuits, and old Tommie R—, a long, lean specimen of Rebeldom, was stretching out his bony arms for the biggest one in the pile, when a minnie ball took off a piece of his head as big as a five-dollar Confederate note, and pitched him over upon our stock of biscuits. George H— jerked at him and cried out: "Damn it, boys, don't let the old man bleed on the biscuts."

F. J. MASON.

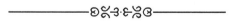

MRS. RICHARD LEDBETTER
By Mrs. K. D. Goodbar, of Charleston

Mrs. Richard Ledbetter is now past seventy years of age. She is a ruddy-cheeked, sunny-natured old lady, whose perfect health is a fair sample of the blessings vouchsafed to those who take a cheery view of life under any and all circumstances. She is always to be met with at the re-union of Confederate soldiers which occurs annually on or about August 2, near Charleston, Arkansas, which is, a notable gathering, sometimes bringing as many as ten thousand people together. Her liveliest memories cluster about the circumstances of a long and wearying journey, which she and a Mrs. Graham made together, during the troublous war times. They rode horseback, entirely without other escort, from a point in Sevier County to Montgomery County, Arkansas, and back again, a total distance of about three hundred miles. Mrs. Graham went for the purpose of nursing a wounded husband, but Private Graham had stepped his last to the drumbeat, and his widow was left only the mournful consolation of a visit to his grave.

Young Mrs. Ledbetter left Mrs. Graham at this point and went on alone, ten miles further, to visit her parents, after which they retraced together the long and dangerous journey.

Both going and coming there seemed an ample opportunity for undesirable adventures, but fortunately they met none of the enemy, and the well-known, undeviating hospitality of the South, afforded them all the shelter and assistance needed. Once only did native intuition, or a special providence, seem to intervene in their behalf when they were led to make a wide detour from the main road and upon rejoining the highway, were told of a large body of Federals, about 500 in number, having passed in the interim. They thus missed an encounter which would have been unpleasant and detaining, to say the least.

———————⊗ℨ·3·ℰ·ℨ⊛———————

UNPRINTED ARKANSAS HISTORY
By Mrs. L. J. Carmack, of Charleston

Mrs. Carmack remembers the funerals of Generals Styne and McCullough. When a small child, she watched the processions march past her father's house in Fort Smith, en route for the National Cemetery.

One of the three soldiers whom three young ladies buried, near Charleston, was shot down in Mrs. Roberts' yard. Mrs. Lizzie Haynes was one of these young ladies. They could not procure coffins for the soldiers, but reverently buried them as best they could, with their own hands. When the sad task was done and they turned homeward, which was three miles distant, the stars were beginning to shine.

Once old Mrs. Susan Richardson and "Grandma" Gunter drove some yearlings hitched to a wagon from Charleston to Fort Smith for provisions. On the way home some of the yearlings became exhausted and the women took turns helping draw the wagon.

The ladies met at the Methodist church in Fort Smith, and made clothes, shirts mostly, for the soldiers.

A Mrs. Beard cut the clothes, and let Mrs. Carmack and many other little schoolgirls make little oilcloth haversacks for the soldiers.

Fort Smith depended on Federal wagon trains for supplies. Most people, especially through the country, spun and wove their cloth.

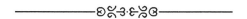

BRAVE AND FEARLESS TO THE END

Miss Pussy Whitty, of Missouri, a plucky and fearless girl of 19, did many acts of daring to decoy the Federals into the hands of her father's company. She went many nights in rain and snow to pilot small bands of Southern patriots and often carried baskets of provisions to the brush to feed the Confederates while recruiting in her State. In the summer of 1863 she rode sixty miles in the night to carry news to the intrepid Quantrell.

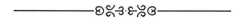

REMINISCENCES OF MRS. VIRGINIA CLEAVER
By Mrs. Virginia C. Cleaver, of Camden

In the fall of 1861, my husband, Capt. W. H. Cleaver, raised a company of cavalry in Homer, Angelina County, Tex. He was in Riley's regiment, Sibley's brigade, and went from Homer to San Antonio, and from there he went on that ill-fated expedition to

New Mexico. He never returned from New Mexico. For many long years of anxiety and suspense—many long years of alternate hope and doubt—I watched for his return and listened for some tidings of him, but it was all in vain. I heard he was killed by Mexicans, July 1, 1862, while crossing the Rio Grande. His horse was shot from under him and fell. He fought bravely for his life, standing in the river, until he fell to rise no more.

After my husband's departure from Homer I remained a week or so in Texas, and then returned by private conveyance to my old home in Arkansas, where lived my widowed mother, one sister and two little brothers. My two older brothers joined the army in the beginning of the war, and the third brother, a mere boy, went a little later. My mother, Mrs. Newport Bragg, lived four miles west of Camden, and as soldiers belonging to both the Confederate and Federal armies were stationed in Camden at different times during the war, we were in the lines of first one army and then the other. When our boys were in possession of Camden it was a gay town, filled with officers, their wives and daughters. So many brave and gallant soldiers with their gray uniforms, the bands playing "Dixie," and "The Bonny Blue Flag," and our loved flag displayed all over the town. Gens. Price and Marmaduke were here, Shelby and his brigade, and many others that I cannot now recall.

We suffered many hardships and privations, but it was all done very cheerfully. Provisions were very scarce, and it was hard to feed our families and our servants, but we always had enough to give to a Confederate soldier. No one who "wore the gray" was ever sent away hungry from my mother's door.

WHEN CLOTHING WAS SCARCE

Clothing was very scarce. A calico dress was a luxury, costing more than a silk one does now, and, like all Southern ladies, we were proud of our homespun dresses. Our hats were made of the palmetto that grows in the swamps. It was cut down, boiled and then bleached in the sun until almost snow white. It was split fine and braided and sewed into a hat. The girls grew very expert in braiding palmetto and the hats were very beautiful. Our shoes we had to make ourselves of various kinds of cloth, most often of gray jeans. We made the uppers, and then had them soled by a shoemaker. We made caps for our soldier boys of grey jeans, and I have made many a pair of gauntlet gloves of dressed fawn silk. I couldn't weave, but my mother had learned to weave when a girl, and she wove my sister and myself some beautiful homespun dresses. She had all the cotton cloth for our servants woven on our farm by a woman belonging to us, and there were several persons in the neighborhood who wove the woolen cloth we needed.

We had no coffee (real coffee, I mean), so had to use various substitutes, such as sweet potatoes, cut, dried and then parched, burnt molasses, parched meal and rye, etc. Our soldiers, who were camped near us for some time, were so good to my mother, who missed her coffee more than the rest of us, that they often saved their entire rations of coffee instead of drinking it themselves and brought it to my mother. Sometimes there would be hardly a teacup of it, tied up in the corner of a much soiled handkerchief, but it was coffee, and we were glad to get it; and after washing it well before roasting it, we enjoyed it very much.

Drugs were very scarce, and we learned to depend on home remedies. For instance, for chills we used tea made of willow bark fodder. A teaspoonful of cornmeal in a little water was taken at intervals, like we do quinine, and strange to say, that often kept off the chill. We learned to do without many things that now are a necessity, and it was cheerfully done, though sometimes the flesh would grow weary and sigh for the "fleshpots of Egypt." There was no sacrifice too great to make for our country and our boys in gray.

CLASH OF PICKETS AT CAMDEN

In '64, when Steele's army was in Camden, there was a picket fight in our yard. Our pickets were stationed a mile east of us, and had a fight with a detachment of Steele's army. Our pickets fell back into our back yard and took refuge behind the house, outbuildings and large trees. My mother and myself got behind a stack chimney in the dining room for safety, and my sister and sister-in-law, who lived with us, hid in a closet to keep from being hit by balls. A ball did come through a window in the dining room and went into the wall about eight feet from where my mother and I were standing.

BATTLES CHEROKEES IN WAR PAINT

Our main army was camped a mile back on the "Two Bayous," and our pickets fell back there. Col. Battle with his regiment of Indians (mostly Cherokees), belonging to Maxey's brigade, came up as quickly as possible, coming through our back yard, and the Yankees seeing them and thinking our main army was behind them, left and were soon at Camden. One of them told me they came out with orders to burn our dwelling, as they had heard of it in Little Rock as being "a regular Secesh harbor." The Indians had on their war paint, and heads decked with peacock feathers. While they were camped at the "Two Bayous," the Indians frequently came to our house for something to eat, and enjoyed the lye hominy and sassafras tea that we had to give them. After eating a plate piled up with the hominy, they would pass the plates back, saying "load up, load up," and we did "load up" in a hurry, for we were afraid of them. Hominy among Indians is called Tom Fuller and is a favorite Indian dish.

The feathers they had came out of our peacock fly brush. An Indian saw it one day, and demanded a feather. Of course he got it. Then another came and still another with the same demand and so on until there was not one left. Perhaps some of the younger generation do not know what a fly brush is. Every Southern household had a brush made of the beautiful iridescent feathers of the peafowl and at meal times in warm weather, a little darky kept the flies off by gently waving it to and fro over the table.

All of our valuables were hidden out from the house and one of our servants, my mother's foreman, assisted in concealing them. A Confederate captain said to my mother one day, "Madam, you had better send that old man back where your other servants are, for if the Yankees come he will surely betray your confidence." She had so much faith in him, that she called him to her and said, "Billy, would you betray the hiding places of my valuables to the Yankees if they come?"

He replied, "Missus, I don't know, I will have to pray over that, before I can tell you," so he was sent down on Red River where the other darkies were.

We had all of our meat hidden out in the woods in a large pen, and the meat was covered with corn, so we would not be left entirely without provisions if the Yankees came, and we flattered ourselves that it was so securely hidden, no one could ever find the pen. One day three Yankees rode up from the direction of the hidden meat and corn. One of them remained at the gate holding the horses and two came in and asked my mother if that was her provisions hidden in the woods. She thinking they were only trying to find out if she had anything concealed, replied, "no," then with an aggravated, tantalizing look one said, "Madam, if it is not yours we will send out and get it tomorrow," she said, "all right," and at the same time her face turned scarlet and the man said, "Ah, madam, your face betrays you; you are not accustomed to telling untruths," but they did not send for it, as the woods were filled with our Soldiers, and they were afraid.

TRAGEDY OF THE TROUSERS

One day when Steele's army was in Camden and our pickets were at our house, there was a poor sick soldier in our barn who sent a friend with a piece of cloth alike on both sides to ask the ladies to make him a pair of trousers. My mother cut them and my sister-in-law and I made them, every stitch being taken with our fingers. He was in a great hurry for them, as he was not presentable, and frequently sent his friend in to hurry us up. Sister J— took one leg and I the other to make. Finally, they were done except putting together, when we found to our dismay they were both made for the same leg. I was not so neat with my needle as my sister, so my part of the work had to be taken out and made over.

When our men were engaged in battle with Steele's army at Poison Springs we could hear the roar of cannon and small arms and see the smoke, as Poison Springs was not more than seven or eight miles distant. After the battle of Prairie d' Anne, Steele's army came to Camden; it was the 15th of April, '64, a bright, beautiful day, and we could hear the rumble of their wagons, twelve hundred in number, for miles.

After many privations and sorrows, the war closed and our boys all came home safely. We were without a dollar, our negroes were freed, our horses and mules had either been "pressed" or confiscated. We had no hogs, no poultry except one old turkey hen that had stolen a nest in the woods and so escaped. A Confederate soldier gave us a poor, old mule, before the surrender and for safety we had it tied to a tree in the back yard, but lightning struck the tree one day and killed it, so then we were, like so many of our Southern people, with only our land left. But our boys were young and hopeful, and took up the burden of life anew, and have succeeded in making a living.

WORK OF CAMDEN WOMEN
By Mrs. G. N. Stinson, of Camden

Maj. Joseph Graham and his charming family were well-known in Camden in the times before the war as leaders in society. Their wealth, education and prominence made the old Graham mansion a notable place. Maj. Graham was a first cousin of Mrs. Stonewall Jackson, and his wife was Mary Washington, who inherited the blood of her kinsmen, George Washington and Robert E. Lee.

The first company of Confederate soldiers to leave Camden, in 1861, was the Camden Knights. They were assigned to the First Arkansas Regiment and were ordered to far-off Virginia. Fathers, husbands and brothers of the principal families were on the roll of this company, and it was a sad trial to the dear ones left behind that two or three weeks were necessary to convey a letter to or fro. But soon other companies were formed and ordered to different commands.

CONFEDERATE SOLDIERS' AID SOCIETY

The ladies of Camden, after bidding adieu to their loved ones, dried their tears and began the life that has endeared the Southern woman to the old Confederate soldier. A society was organized to make clothes for the soldiers, gather medicines and write them cheering letters. Mrs. J. H. Graham was chosen president and soon became the guiding light. The writer was a member of that society and well remembers the perfect unity that prevailed, notwithstanding the fact that all religious denominations and all classes of society were represented.

Mrs. Graham gave freely of her money and her time. She fed the hungry, clothed the threadbare and nursed the sick back to life. Two soldiers died in her home, whom she had nursed as tenderly as their mother could have done.

MAKING CLOTHES

Whole suits of clothes and undergarments were made by ladies who had not previously ever made one. A tailor or skilled woman in cutting was employed to cut out garments, which were frequently taken home to be returned in a few days. Many, however, preferred to work at the society meetings and exchange the news and gossip of the day.

The woods were scoured for roots and barks to dye the Confederate gray. They resurrected the spinning wheel, carded and spun.

KNITTING SOCKS FOR PRICE'S BODYGUARD

Knitting socks—this was the most fashionable work of the times, the old teaching the young. Women walked the streets of Camden knitting socks, and on a visit to a friend the click of the knitting needles kept time with their tongues.

General Sterling Price's bodyguard, one frosty morning, halted long enough at Mrs. Graham's to receive eighty pairs of socks. Mrs. Caroline Burk knitted a sock one day that a poor Confederate soldier might have two pairs as he was hurriedly ordered away. Mrs. Tyra Hill knitted a pair of socks as she rode in her carriage from Camden to Washington on a visit to her son.

These women had been delicately reared, but they remembered that they were Southern women and that the South had now need of their work. They frequently toiled all day and far into the night, so that some passing soldier might be cared for or the box for their distant loved ones made ready.

HOSPITAL WORK

The sick and wounded soldiers were cared for in Camden. There were regular days to send nourishing and dainty meals to the sick and other days to visit them and cheer them up. For those at a distance, bed comforts and food that would keep good for a few days would be shipped as circumstances permitted, and many a soldier exhibited in camp the handiwork of the wife, mother or the girl he left behind him.

WHEN HOPE HAD FLED

The women had nobly done their part at home as the men had done theirs on the field of battle. But in 1865 all hope had fled, and the tattered remnants came back. The returning soldier many times found his old home in ruins but his wife was not sitting a picture of desolation bemoaning her sad lot. The women did not complain or censure. They spoke words of cheer and comfort to their brave soldiers and when the white wings of peace rested on our Southland, they took up their new tasks with renewed vigor, assisting their dear men to mend their broken fortunes.

But few are now living that helped Mrs. Graham to pack boxes of clothing for the boys in gray. Mr. and

Mrs. Graham and six children are sleeping in the old Camden cemetery. Only one child survives them, Mrs. Laura Toney of Woodberry, Ark., a worthy descendant of a noble family.

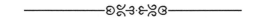

WOULD NEVER LOVE ANOTHER COUNTRY

This is one of Gen. Gordon's stories: In the Confederate army Longstreet's corps was making a night march. About 3 or 4 o'clock in the morning when everyone was tired and worn out, a Georgia regiment stopped. A Georgia soldier put his rifle up against the tents on the other side of where Longstreet was. "Well," he said, "this is pretty hard—to fight all day and march all night. But I suppose I can do it for my country." He continued: "I can go hungry, I can fight; if need be I can die for my country, because I love my country; but when this war is over I'll be blowed if I'll ever love another country."

—Christian Register.

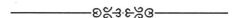

REMINISCENCES OF MRS. E. S. SCOTT
By Mrs. A. A. Tufts, of Camden

The name of my mother, Mrs. E. S. Scott of Camden, may be very properly enrolled among the number of those who loved and suffered for the South. Though she was mercifully spared the crowning blow which fell upon so many other mothers, whose brave sons gave up their lives in the struggle, yet she worked faithfully and spent many an hour of keen suspense and shed many bitter tears during those four long years. At first, she was opposed to secession, on account of the terrors of war, but when Virginia, her native state, and Arkansas, her home state, went out of the Union, Mother went too, and when my brothers took up arms against the North she was ready with heart and tongue, pen and prayers, to further the cause. She was naturally of a bright and cheery disposition, especially fond of the society of young people, and once she laughingly said, "I might have stayed young always and never had to wear glasses, if it had not been for Abe Lincoln and his war making me shed so many tears and read by tallow candles."

With the other ladies of Camden she was daily to be found sewing for the soldiers, knitting socks or rolling bandages. In a letter, dated August 15, 1861, she writes as follows: "We have a Soldiers' Aid society and are working constantly. We are determined to sustain our soldiers as far as we are able, to work for them, pray for them, and if the worst comes, we will burn up our houses and sweep the earth literally and die, before we will give up our fair and beautiful land."

O! that victory at Manassas! The God of Israel was and is our God. Glory be to His holy name!" Early in the war the regiment to which my brothers belonged were engaged east of the Mississippi River, and in order to be near them my mother went to Gainesville, Ala., where she lived the greater part of the time until the surrender. Then she began to work for the soldiers in a way very near to her heart. There was a

Confederate military hospital in the town, under the charge of Dr. Randolph Brunson, late of Pine Bluff, and I well remember how enthusiastically she took up the work of nursing the sick and wounded soldiers. It was very hard to procure good brandy and nourishing food, but she always managed in some way to get the very best in the hospital stores for her special patients. At one time we had three sick soldiers in our house, of whom she had entire care. One was my oldest brother, Capt. Frank T. Scott, who had some serious eye trouble; another was Lieut. McLaughlin, with a shattered leg, and the third was a young Virginian, A. P. Bierne, midshipman in the Confederate navy, suffering from the results of exposure, which threatened consumption.

During the summer of 1863, my mother was in Yazoo City, Miss., where the cannonading at Vicksburg could be plainly heard. My younger brother, Capt. C. C. Scott, was in the besieged city, and it was a time of great anxiety to my mother. Some of the days when the cannonading was constant she would often say, "It may be that shot has killed my boy." Then again on a day when all was still there would come the fear that the city had surrendered and she would almost long to hear again the roar of the cannon.

In Yazoo City the court house was used as a military hospital, and I can remember going there with mother and seeing the sick men on cots even out in front on the sidewalk. One day the news came that Federal troops were entering the city, and mother was greatly distressed to see the pale, emaciated men put into rude conveyances and hurried away for fear of capture.

Soon after the surrender we returned to our home near Camden where for a year or two afterward mother still had a soldier to care for. This was a one-armed Confederate, who began to build up his fortune as a farmer, and who had the misfortune to break two fingers on his only hand. For several months it was her self-appointed task to dress and care for his crippled hand, and sometimes with eyes so misty with tears that she could scarcely see how to apply the dressings properly. She was more fortunate than many mothers in this, that both of her sons were spared to return home and be a comfort to her for the 11 years that she lived after the war closed, and when at last she came to the end of her pilgrimage she was ready to lay down the burden she had borne so patiently and her beautiful, faithful and gentle life will ever remain an inspiration, not only to her children, but to all who ever came within the sphere of her influence.

Few people living now have any idea what heroism it required to be a Confederate mother. They lived in a state of constant apprehension, fear of death or wounds to their soldier boys at the front and fear of starvation and rags for the little ones at home. Every strange face and every letter brought a chill to the heart. Eagerly they listened for news from the front, though at the same time dreading to hear what was oftener bad news than good. They toiled and slaved and comforted each other during the day, but at night while their little ones slept, their pillows were wet with tears as they wept and prayed with none but the great God to listen to their sobbing.

PRAYER OF MRS. HOOD MOVING
FEDERAL RAIDERS
By Mrs. S. Hood, of Camden

I was 17 years old when the war commenced and had been married a year. We had a happy home in Camden, Ark. My husband, four brothers and two brother-in-laws joined the Confederate regiment that was made up there. They were in many battles, but none was killed or even wounded, except one, who received a flesh wound in his arm. With one exception, an old and broken down man, all are now dead.

HUSBAND'S UNEXPECTED RETURN

My husband had been gone two years, and not hearing from him, I thought that he was dead. One evening I was weaving cloth. The loom house was about three feet above the ground and there were no steps. My ear, alert to every footstep, caught that of my husband. I jumped fully five feet to get to him. We were now happy for a time. His health was broken down and just as soon as he was able to handle a musket off he went again.

FEDERAL RAIDERS MOVED BY PRAYER

I was living across the Ouachita River when the Federals came to Camden. I had a good horse and hid him and everything else that could be carried away. A neighbor of mine was not so fortunate. She was a widow and her sons were in the Southern army.

I happened to be at her house one day when 200 Federals rode up. It was noon and they wanted dinner. The poor woman fed as many as she could. They went searching all over the place for meat, lard and bread-stuffs. Then they tried to find the horses. They asked where her husband was and she told them that she was a widow. Then they wanted to know whether any of her boys were rebel soldiers, and when she replied "yes," they began cursing at a fearful rate.

That poor widow, believing that her last hour had come, fell upon her knees and poured forth such a prayer as I had never before or since heard. It moved those rough men so that some of them actually cried and they declared that the prayer would last them their lifetime. The whole troop soon left her in peace. Two of her sons died in the war and now she, too, has gone to her reward.

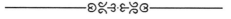

CARRYING OUT HIS ORDERS

Hugh Mc—, a son of the Emerald Isle, who had volunteered in the 6th South Carolina infantry, was stationed on the beach of Sullivan's Island with strict orders to let no one pass him without the countersign, and that to be communicated only in a whisper. Two hours later the corporal, with the relief, discovered by the moonlight Hugh, up to his waist in water, the tide having set in since he was posted.

"Who goes there?" the sentinel shouted.

"Relief."

"Halt relief. Advance corporal and give the counter-sign."

"I'm not going in there to be drowned," replied the corporal. "Come out here and let me relieve you."

"Divil a bit of it," returned Hugh. "The leftenant toald me not to lave me post."

"Well, then," replied the corporal, "I'll leave you in the water all night," and he turned as he spoke.

But the sentinel's gun was promptly cocked and levelled.

"Halt. I'll put a hole in you ef ye pass without the countersign. Them's me orders from the leftenant."

"Confound you," cried the corporal, "everybody will hear it if I bawl it out to you."

"Yes, me darlin," rejoined Hugh, "and the leftenant said it must be given in a whisper. In with ye. Me finger's on the trigger and me gun may go off."

The corporal yielded to this and waded in to the faithful sentinel, who exclaimed: "Be jabbers, it's well you've come—the bloody tide has most drowned me."

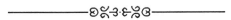

RECOLLECTIONS OF MRS. M. C. HINES, OF CAMDEN

When I look back through the lapse of some forty-odd years, back through the dark days that looked then like ruin and disaster, back through the days of pilfering and plundering, back through the events of the bloody, unjust strife, when this Southland was filled with guerrillas, jayhawkers, carpetbaggers and blood-sucking vampires, I feel almost appalled at the circumstances and conditions existing in those passing events of that just and nobly fought cause. I am seventy-four years old and can't say that I feel my infirmities. My health is fairly good. My hearing and eyesight is almost as good as it was thirty years ago. I enjoy life yet, enjoy church going and visiting my neighbors. My scope in this life has been one of broad measure, and when I view the lost cause in its original latitude and longitude "so to speak," I feel that I won as great a battle as any, or almost any of the sons of our Southland. Being deprived of the care, comfort and support of my husband, whose name was Wm. Lafayette Hines, who died in July, 1863, being left with three little children to care for, to be mother and father too, I kept my vigil as does the good angel on the death watch of an infant child. I lost my home, which in its true sense means a great deal. Lost my kindred relatives and friends, lost everything, but clung to my little ones. I was mother, wife and landlord; had to chop wood, make fires, cook, plow, hoe, card, spin and weave, running the whole gauntlet, filling all the life's offices, dreading nightfall with all its hideous affliction, and I almost feel the chilly sensations yet. Expecting to be disturbed by some prowling marauder or listening for the clatter of some Yankee's horses feet or probably listening to the welcome "hoo hoo" of a friendly owl; singing a cradle lullaby to my children until tired and worn out. When I would lay me down to sleep, knowing not whether I would wake or be murdered or burned alive. It was about this wise that I spent that never-to-be-forgotten period which is as fresh in my memory today as the living sun.

FEDERAL RAIDERS
By Mrs. Laitra A. Wooten, of Corsicana

My veins are chilled when I think of the privations endured during the civil war period. I married R. C. Brazel, 18 miles south of Camden two years before the war began. Our home was a farm. My husband joined General Tappan Grinstead's regiment and was made first lieutenant in 1861. A little girl had been born to us and six months after my husband's departure a little boy came. My father, Rev. William Winburne of the Little Rock conference, died in December, 1862, and my mother came to live with me. Her house and all its contents were destroyed by fire and she had the misfortune of breaking her arm in her efforts to escape.

FEDERAL SOLDIERS PLUNDER

Three weeks after the fire, the enemy came and took every horse that mother and I had. They took our meat and plundered the house generally. Mother remonstrated a little, telling them that she was a poor widow with two girls to take care of and they called her a liar! They then turned their attention to me, asking where my husband was. I replied that he was in the Confederate army where I wanted him to be.

DID NOT EVEN SPARE THE BLIND

They spread general devastation. One incident will do to explain all. My father-in-law Brazel was totally blind. They went to his home, took every horse, stripped the beds, stole the dishes from the pantry and then went to the smoke house and after taking the meat emptied three or four barrels of flour on the floor and mixed in a barrel of molasses. They ordered our negro cook to prepare dinner and tried to induce her to run away with them. She refused. Then they plundered her house and took things of no earthly use to them.

I hope that there will be no more war in my lifetime. The incidents that I have narrated are only a few of those that remain stamped on my memory. Why the great army of the North should have made war upon women and children is hard to understand.

————————

RELIGIOUS "LOYALTY"

This explains itself:

Headquarters Norfolk and Portsmouth.
Norfolk, Va., Feb. 11, 1864.

General Orders No. 3:

All places of public worship in Norfolk and Portsmouth are hereby placed under the control of the provost marshals of Norfolk and Portsmouth, respectively, who shall see the pulpits properly filled by displacing, when necessary, the present incumbents and substituting men of known loyalty and the same sectional denomination, either military or civil, subject to the approval of the commanding general.

They shall see that the churches are open freely to all officers and soldiers, white or colored, at the usual hour of worship, and at other times, if desired, and they shall see that no insult or indignity be offered to them, either by word, look or gesture on the part of the congregation.

The necessary expenses will be levied as far as possible in accordance with the previous usage or regulations of each congregation respectively.

No property shall be removed, either public or private, without permission from these headquarters.

By command of Brigadier-General E. A. WILDE,

GEORGE H. JOHNSON,
Captain and Assistant Adjutant-General.

Headquarter's Provost Marshal's Office,
Norfolk, Va., Feb. 13, 1864.

Any insult, indignities or abuse offered to officers or soldiers visiting houses of worship under the above order, should be reported at once to this office.

CHARLES M. WHELDEN.
Lieutenant-Colonel and Provost
Marshal, District of Virginia.

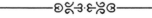

WHEN PAPA WAS GONE TO THE WAR
By Mrs. L. A. Eason, of De Queen

My father, Dorton Clark, was a Confederate soldier and served through the war. When papa went to the war, mamma was left to provide for four little girls. The times were so hard that she had no shoes for her feet. By working hard every day she was able to keep a roof over our heads. Roasting ears were a welcome food. Roasted potatoes and boiled vegetables, with only salt to season them, were our food. There was no meat. Sassafras tea and coffee made from potatoes were our drink. We children picked the cotton from the seed with our fingers, and mamma spun and wove the cloth, so that we might have some clothing.

FATHER DOWN WITH RHEUMATISM

When papa came home after the war, he was struck down with rheumatism. He lived until January 18, 1904, but was able to do very little work. The cost of his medical attendance and of his funeral ate up mother's little savings. Mother was 70 years old March 28, 1907. She does not regret or repine over the past. She is a true Southern woman, as my father was a true Southern man.

—————————⊙℥᠄ɜ·ɛ·℥⊙—————————

INCIDENT IN THE LIFE OF MRS. C. K. HOLMAN
By Miss Ida C. Holman, of De Queen

Not having any recollection of the war myself, I send a little circumstance which I have often heard my mother, now dead, relate. I have often heard her say that she never refused a Confederate soldier food or shelter and never charged one for it, and was never treated with any discourtesy by one. I have also heard her and other women in this county say that they fared worse after the war, during the reconstruction period, about 1868, when the militia were in this county, than they did during the war.

During the absence of her husband in the army, Mrs. C. K. Holman, then living near Paracliffta, Sevier County, Ark., was one night requested by some Confederate soldiers to furnish them food and lodgings for the night, which she cheerfully did. Among them was a young soldier who reminded her of one of her own sons, then far away from home. While sitting around the fire after supper, she observed a hole in the knee of the trousers of the young soldier, and after the men had retired she sent her son to the room to tell the young man that if he would send his trousers to her she would mend them. On hearing this message to the young man, all of the others exclaimed, "Take mine, too! Take mine, too!" which he did, and as there were quite a number of them, Mrs. Holman and her daughter (now Mrs. Sager of Hubbard, Tex.) sat up nearly all the night repairing them.

I do not claim that there was either heroism or fortitude displayed in this incident; merely a small service, willingly rendered, to some of the men who wore the gray.

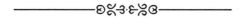

WOMEN PLOWING IN THE FIELD
By Mrs. James, of Doddridge

My husband joined the Confederate army the second year of the war and served until his death. We were living in Forsythe, Ga., at that time. He left me with five little boys.

Although I had plenty of Confederate money, it would not buy anything, and even with gold I had the greatest difficulty in procuring the necessaries of life. To support myself and children I was obliged to plow and hoe all day in the field, and then work a part of the night carding, spinning and weaving wool and cotton, to clothe myself and little ones. In the woods we found herbs that would dye our rough cloth, some for ourselves and some to send to my husband. Our coffee was made from corn meal and tea from sassafras roots. Those were hard times on a woman with no man to advise or help her.

After the Yankees came, there was new money, greenbacks, and some five and ten-cent shinplasters. As the money would buy something, and as there were occasionally sutler stores in the Federal army where purchases might be made, I sold a few geese and was able to obtain some very necessary articles.

RAIDING PARTIES OF BOTH ARMIES

The advance of the Federal army did not always mean a permanent stay. The Federals came frequently as a raiding party and would retire upon the advance of a Confederate force, which had also no intention of remaining permanently. The Federals were enemies, but the Confederates were often in desperate need of horses, forage and food. War also dulled the sensibilties of men. They became used to pillage and a weak woman's voice was not heard. A raiding party of one side would come one week, to be followed by a scouting party of the other side. We hid our horses in the forest thickets and they found them saddled and bridled. These raiders robbed our beegums, took all the food in sight. I have stood in my yard and heard the cannons roar and the small arms crackle, as a skirmish or battle began. My husband was in a distant command, and under all the sad circumstances that surrounded my life I sometimes wished that the battle roar that fell upon my ears was the death knell of the war.

NOW 73 YEARS OLD

I am now 73 years old and have been for many years a resident of Arkansas. The Confederate Pension Board of the State upon a consideration of the changed circumstances of my life and perhaps the fidelity with which I have tried to uphold the character of a Southern woman, granted me a pension in 1904, of $48. I appreciate the kindness of the Pension Board. It makes an old woman feel good to know that her husband's army life and her own sacrifices during the Civil War are not forgotten.

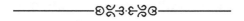

GRAND ROUNDS

There happened to be on post one night in Arkansas a Frenchman by the name of Victor Pedron, as gallant a Confederate as ever shouldered a musket. He was on the second relief and toward the close of his tour was getting tired and sleepy, when to his great joy, he saw a body of men approaching, which he did not doubt was the third relief. "Who comes dere?" he called. "Grand rounds," was the reply. "Begar, I thought it was ze tird relief," returned the disappointed sentinel, and then nothing further being said, the group advanced, rousing the weary sentinel again: "Who comes, dere?" Again was repeated, "Grand rounds." But this time the irritated man could not contain himself and half asleep shouted: "Oh, go vay wid your grand rounds. I have ze grand sommeil."

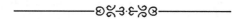

SOUTHERN WOMEN WALKING FIFTY MILES TO MILL AND CARRYING SACKS OF MEAL BACK HOME
By E. E. Collier, near Dardanelle

Before the Federals occupied this country, I had accumulated a large amount of corn and wheat. To show the condition the country was in, I can truthfully say that for over two years I never saw a man come to the mill except armed squads of scouts, and not customers. Our customers were women altogether. I have seen as many as forty-six women at the mill at one time waiting their turns. Some came as far as thirty-five and forty miles. Two women would get two wagon wheels, sometimes one would belong to the front and the other to the hind part of the wagon. Then they would yoke up two yearling steers, and put a line on each one. One woman on the right side and the other on the left to hold the cattle in the road, and drive to mill and back again with their load. Often they came without any grain but none ever went away without breadstuff. Again some would bring two or maybe three yards of home made cotton cloth to pay for their meal or flour. The price was a dollar a yard. Those who came a long distance and had to stay all night were always taken to our house. Women came in bunches from Dover in Pope County and crossed the Arkansas River; from Lanes Bottom; from Johnson County and from Scott County. A party of thirteen women came once from Scott County, some fifty miles or more on foot and each one got all she could carry on her back. Many women once in good circumstances were reduced to this extremity.

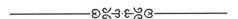

BLOODY WORK OF BUSHWHACKERS IN YELL COUNTY AND NEAR POCAHONTAS
By Mrs. L. C. Hall, of Dardanelle

Situated between two armies and being frequently overrun by the raiding and scouting parties of each,

Yell County suffered much from the horrors of war; but worse than either Federal or Confederate troops, were the depreciations and atrocities of bands of marauders belonging to neither side, known as bushwhackers or jawhawkers, who preyed impartially on secessionist and unionist alike.

From Mrs. Hart, an aged lady now well on between eighty and ninety years of age, and her daughter, Mrs. McCray and Miss Lizzie Hart, I heard many incidents of those perilous times, in which they were active. All men able to bear arms were in the field, only the aged and infirm, and the very young boys being left at home as protectors. Many of these were murdered in cold blood by the bushwhackers and at times it was necessary to preserve their lives, or that they hide from these lawless bands, whose watchword seemed to be "Kill! Kill! Kill!" and whose lust for blood seemed well nigh insatiable.

During one of these seasons of social peril. a young man named Underwood, belonging to Capt. Hollswell's command, was fatally wounded by Jake Graves, a bushwhacker. Under cover of night, he was carried on a stretcher several miles to the banks of Harris Creek, at a point near the Hart home, where he was placed in a tent, concealed by the heavy woods and undergrowth. Here he was nursed, night and day, by six heroic girls, two at a time, for several days until death relieved him of his sufferings. His grave was made on the spot where he died, and he was buried by three old men, Messrs. Toomer, Harrington, and Pendergrass. They dared not mark his grave. but concealed it as well as they could, being assisted by these six young heroines, his faithful nurses, Mrs. McCray, then Miss Anne Hart, her sister,

Miss Lally, afterwards Mrs. Leonard Cotton, Miss Pendergrass, now Mrs. Berry, Misses Harrington and Hoovis, and Miss Ferguson of Pope County; whether or not these three last are living, or whether married or single I know not.

The Hart home was known as Confederate headquarters, and one dark night, word was received that the Federals were coming. There being no other way to warn the small Confederate command of their approach, Miss Lally Hart, a young girl of seventeen, rode through the midnight woods, three or four miles, alone, to give the alarm.

Mrs. Hart, whose mind is wonderfully clear and alert, told of her many experiences, some humorous, as when she became a sort of peripatetic postoffice, using her hose, already fulfilling their lawful function, as mailbags, many otherwise, as when she rode horse-back many perilous miles, with the fear of death in her heart, to carry relief, in the shape of a sack of meal to a starving family. On one occasion, she accompanied the ox wagon, driven by one of her faithful negroes, ten or twelve miles with a load of corn and wheat to be ground at Wood's mill. Part of the load belonged to neighbors, and she hoped by her presence to protect it from thieves. The wheat had been ground and sacked, and was in the upper story of the mill. While the corn was being ground, the Federals rode up to the mill, and immediately confiscated the meal. In vain the lady pleaded for at least a portion of it, to take back to her neighbors who had confided the corn to her care. Not one peck would they allow her. So off they went with the entire amount, including the miller's toll, "but," she added, with a little chuckle of satisfaction, in telling me of it, a few days ago, "they didn't know a thing about the flour upstairs, and you may be sure I didn't tell them."

In an old scrap book belonging to Mrs. Dora Shinn, nee Lemoyne, I find the following taken from "The Pocahontas Herald:"

"Miss Williams, a daughter of Isaac Williams, living in Black River swamp, about seven miles from this place, heard the report that troops were approaching this place on Sunday evening. Her father was not at home, but she immediately caught a horse, and was soon off in search of him.

"She found him at a neighbor's and told him to hurry on home and get his gun, and come here to help drive back the enemy. She then returned home, got down her father's rifle, moulded all his lead into bullets, took the gun, powder and bullets, and hid them under the house, again mounted the horse, and rode to several houses and spread the alarm, returning home in time to give the old man his gun and ammunition and started him with a crowd of ten men she had collected for the scene of action. All this she did in less than two hours. Such acts of heroism should not be passed by without notice.

This same scrap-book has this comment on the weather:

"The weather is as cold as a Yankee's heart, and as disagreeable as his company; as blustering as he is before a battle, and as dismal as he is after one."

There are many newspaper accounts of battles, with private letters from soldiers, on the same subjects which the papers were permitted to print. There was also the speech of Miss Lucy Lorraine Adams, presenting a flag to the Moro Greys, Calhoun County, and of Miss Elizabeth Higginbotham, presenting a flag to the Jackson Minute Men.

———————————⊗≾⃨3⃨·ε⃨·≾⃨⊗———————————

HOW WOMEN SUPPORTED THE FAMILY
By Mrs. Pattie Wright Hedges, of El Dorado

Many scenes and incidents of my childhood seem written in indelible letters on my brain. Of these, the civil war period has perhaps the most conspicuous place. In truth I set out on life's voyage under rather sad though thrilling circumstances, since I sat at the feet of my father, and heard his talk to my mother and brothers of war. War! why, what did it mean? I listened breathlessly and in silence to those somewhat excited conversations, nearly every one taking part in them, having some reason to advance or solution to offer, until I slowly and laboriously grasped the thought that for some cause all the men in the entire country had fallen out, had quarreled and forthwith had taken guns and swords in their hands with which to slay one another. In this aspect the struggle appeared in my childish eyes. But ere the four weary years which intervened between 1861 and 1865 had passed, even the children in that part of Arkansas in which I lived, knew but too well the meaning of war, and became familiar, too, with its attendant sorrow, suffering, privation and death.

My father, Major Edward W. Wright, lived in 1861, in Union County, Arkansas, not far from the little village of Lisbon, and about sixteen miles from El

Dorado. The adjacent country was made up of quite a goodly settlement of wealthy planters. When the war fairly opened, very nearly all the able-bodied men in it forthwith entered the Confederate army.

AN UNPROTECTED COMMUNITY

Thus it fell out that all that portion of Arkansas was virtually left without a man capable of bearing arms, the aged men, women and children, and the negroes, alone making up the remaining population; nor was it long before these noncombatants faced conditions which had never before existed for the blockade cut off supplies of all kinds to a great extent, and the capture of New Orleans effectually shut out even the necessaries of life. But some time prior to this latter event, indeed I may say quite soon after the greater part of the men had gone to swell the number of Confederate soldiers, the women of Union County had shown themselves entitled to bear the honorable and worthy names of Spartan wives and mothers. The call of duty found them ready, nor were they daunted in the presence of danger.

The entire county presented a scene of remarkable activity, in which woman was the commanding figure. In the household, in the workshop, on the plantation, the hand of woman was displayed; and woman's mind, directed nearly every undertaking, great or little. Perhaps on the different plantations was her work more highly appreciated and more beneficial, for here with their own hands, aided of course by slaves, the women raised supplies, not only for the subsistence of their immedate households and those dependent upon them, but also for the armies of the Southland. So long as the troops were in the state, little difficulty was experienced in getting provisions and articles of clothing to them, but when the army was beyond the Mississippi, many obstacles were encountered, some of which it was found impossible to overcome.

It must not be imagined that the production of these supplies was accomplished without vast trouble, and many hardships. Yet withall there was no faltering on the part of these heroic women. What tongue or pen can portray or describe the sacrifices they made, the sufferings they endured in the dark days of 1862 and 1865? I feel inadequate to the task of attempting at best a feeble recital of their lot at that particular time, yet I shall try to record, or at least give a glimpse of some things they accomplished under circumstances that must have tried the stoutest heart, the loftiest courage.

My information was given me some years ago, nearly all of those who supplied it having long since gone to their eternal reward; and I have treasured it both for the memory which it embalms as well as its value to the future historian. From it I learn how the country comprising and surrounding the home of my childhood was almost in a day transformed from a land of opulence and luxury, a land "flowing with milk and honey," into a section where care and toil took up their abode, and where the very trees, shrubs and flowers were prized not so much for their beauty, fragrance and appearance, as for their medicinal qualities, or their power to supply, though in the slightest degree, food or raiment for human kind.

WOMAN'S AID TO CONFEDERACY

The uniforms for the first company of Confederate soldiers that left Union County were made by women who met at El Dorado, where nimble and willing fingers, though unused to that sort of work, quickly fashioned the cloth which a tailor had cut into garbs for the soldier boys. And this was only the beginning, since thenceforward this and other kinds of labor was carried forward altogether by women. Looms, tanneries, spinning wheels were kept busily employed, the most of the products thereof being sent to the army, though in various shapes and guises. A common purpose inspired all, wealth, station, rank, being forgotten in the desire to aid the Confederacy. Plants and shrubs heretofore of little value suddenly became of the greatest use. Boneset, Horehound, Mullen, each had its particular sphere at that time. But the Poppy was of the highest benefit. The seed was sown generally in the garden; when the plant reached a certain age an incision was made in the stalk with a sharp knife, and the sap oozed out in the form of a gum, which was dried and used in lieu of opium. It was put in boxes or small packages and sent to the various hospitals. Indigo was likewise largely cultivated, and was employed in dyeing cloth. Beef tallow was held in high esteem, especially by those who, like my mother, were so fortunate as to own a pair of candle moulds, for a supply of candles was extremely desirable. The more general way of supplying light for the household was to take several yards of wicking, which had been spun soft, doubled and twisted, wax it and soak it in turpentine, then take a bottle, wind the wicking around it, leaving a little at the top to be lighted, and as it burnt down, pull the wicking up. Scores of women served by this sort of light, making, clothing for the soldiers and for members of their household, and thought themselves lucky.

But the contents of the boxes which were sent from time to time to the soldiers in the field, showed more clearly the result of women's labor, and the various expedients which changed conditions had forced them to adopt. For the box contained many suits of jeans, home-made blankets usually made from carpets taken from the floors of parlors and sitting-rooms, shoes of various sizes, home-made handkerchiefs, pin cushions filled with pins and needles, sewing thread, towels, soap both to use in washing face and body, and also to put in the soldier's socks to prevent the feet from blistering while on a long march, boxes of different kinds of salves, corn cob pipes with bits of cane for stems, sacks of red pepper for seasoning food and also to put in soldier's shoes or boots to keep his feet warm, scores of black balls made of bees-wax with which to color white thread, rice, home-grown and husked in a mortar made from a tree whose length been burnt into a cone-shaped hole, the pestle composed of a piece of wood with nails driven in the end. There was something for every member of the company, no one being overlooked or forgotten. And each box had many rolls of linen for bandages made from bed linen, and lint scraped, oh, how carefully, from table linen and pillow cases. Aside from these things there were socks, underclothing, and scores of smaller articles, all of which were of use and value in the camp. Nor must I forget a stock of stationery, made of all kinds and colors of wrapping paper, dingy and brown perhaps, but nevertheless very acceptable to the soldier to whom it was sent; and with it were goose quills for pens, and many bottles of home-made ink. Furthermore, there were boxes specially prepared for the sick and for the hospitals, containing many delicacies, such as coffee, tea, and other things that had been stored away with all a miser's care for just such purposes, that is to say for the sick and wounded soldiers. These boxes were usually sent by wagons to Camden and thence to Memphis, from whence they were forwarded to their destination. Later when the Federal authority gained control of the last named place, other sources were found whereby to reach the Southern army. For until the last the women never ceased their labors, though hardships and privations encompassed them about.

I have only touched on a portion of the part which the women of Union County, Arkansas, played in the dark and trying days of the Civil war. But I most sincerely trust that this imperfect sketch may give some conception, however feeble, of the heroism, the self-sacrificing spirit which inspired the women of the section of the state of which I have written; and that coming generations may recall their labors, sufferings and sacrifices with just pride and profound reverence.

————————ᴐᶽⱻᶽᴆ————————

DISPOSAL OF "REBEL" WOMEN
(Extracts from official orders.)

Headquarter's Seventeenth Army Corps,
Provost Marshal's Office.

Vicksburg, Dec. 27, 1863.

The following named persons, Miss Kate Barnett, Miss Ella Barnett, Miss Laura Latham, Miss Ellie Martin, and Mrs. Mary Moore, having acted disrespectfully towards the president and government of the United States, and having insulted the officers, soldiers and loyal citizens of the United States, who had assembled at the Episcopal church in Vicksburg on Christmas day for divine service, where the officiating minister prays for the welfare of "the president of the United States and all others in authority," are hereby banished and will leave the Federal lines within forty-eight hours, under penalty of imprisonment.

Hereafter all persons, male or female, who by word, deed or implicatioin, do insult or show disrespect to the president, government or flag of the United States or any officer or soldier of the United States, upon matters of a national character, shall be fined, banished or imprisoned, according to the grossness of the offense.

By order of

MAJOR-GENERAL M'PHERSON,
JAMES WILSON, Lieutenant-Colonel,
Provost Marshal, Seventeenth Army
Corps.

FAREWELL TO JACKSONPORT GUARDS
By Mrs. V. Y. Cook, of Elmo

Of all my childhood memories of the war between the North and South, nothing remains so vivid as the words "Roll him in the river," which were spoken by a tall, angular old woman, as she rushed up to a squad of soldiers who were rolling a large box down the river bank.

This incident occurred at Grand Glaize on a beautiful Sunday afternoon early in May, 1861, when the storm cloud of war was beginning to burst over our Southland.

Excitement was high and the hot heads who staid at home were revelling in the notoriety of the occasion.

A week previous to this well remembered day, a stranger made his way unobserved into our little town and upon being questioned refused to give any information regarding himself or his intentions. Of course, he was immediately arrested as a spy, but as nothing definite could be proved, it was decided that he should be caged and sent to Abraham Lincoln. "But before being shipped, he must be "marked," some one suggested. So carrying out this suggestion, half of his beard and half of his hair were shaved off, leaving one side of his face and head perfectly smooth. He was then placed in a large box and put in a prominent place for exhibition until the next boat passed. To the children of the town, he was an object of terror, and all were glad that he had been caught before he had time to do any harm to the Southern Army.

Thus on the day mentioned, a great crowd of people, including our company of soldiers, the Glaize Rifles, in their bright new uniforms lined the bank of the river on each side of the landing to greet and bid farewell to the Jacksonport Guards who were leaving that day for the battlefields of Virginia.

On hearing that a Yankee was boxed ready to be shipped to Lincoln, the Jacksonport Guards begged that he might he put on their boat that they might hang him to the jackstaff before sundown, and without waiting for the consent of the ones in charge, some of them rushed up the street to get the cage, coming back rolling it with the poor old fellow inside as though it were a bale of cotton.

Among those who had come to bid the last farewell to the ones leaving home for the sake of their country, was an old lady whose only son and child was leaving her that day and whom she never expected to see again.

No wonder she cried out, "Roll him in, roll the Yankee in, if it was not for such as he, my son would not be leaving me today."

The caged Yankee was carried to Memphis and there offered his liberty, but enjoying his notoriety, he refused it and was taken as far as Cairo in his box.

——————————ම෪ঽ·ɛঽ෬——————————

LEE'S FAREWELL ADDRESS

Headquarters Army of Northern Virginia, Appomattox
C. H., April 10, 1865.
General Order No. 19.

After four years of arduous service, marked by un-surpassed courage and fortitude, the army of Northern Virginia has been compelled to yield to overwhelming numbers and resources. I need not tell the survivors of so many hard-fought battles, who have remained steadfast to the last, that I have consented to this result from no distrust of them, but feeling that valor and de-votion could accomplish nothing that would compen-sate for the loss that must have attended a continuance of the contest, I determined to avoid the useless sacri-fice of those whose past services have endeared them to their countrymen. By the terms of agreement, officers and men can return to their homes and remain until ex-changed. You will take with you the satisfaction that proceeds from the conciousness of duty well performed, and I earnestly pray that a merciful God will extend to you His blessings and protection. With an unceasing admiration of your constancy and devotion to your country, and a grateful remembrance of your kind and generous consideration for myself, I bid you an affec-tionate farewell.

R E. LEE.

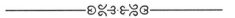

HARDSHIPS OF THE WIFE OF A CAPTAIN IN MONROE'S REGIMENT
By Mrs. D. L. Vance, of Eureka Springs

My husband, D. L. Vance, was captain of Company G, Monroe's regiment, Cabell's brigade. He went to the army the first of the year 1862, and remained in it till he was killed by Union home guards, July, 1864. I lived in the country, about 20 miles below Little Rock. After the Federals took Little Rock it was not long until they began foraging through the country. Several of them passed my house one day, and when they came back they had a drove of cattle. The road ran through our field, and they had two large gates to pass through. Some of my cattle had just come up and I went to drive them out of the way and got all away but one, when the Yankees drove it away from me. I was so angry that I threw the club I had in my hand at one of them. I tried to hit him, but struck his horse in the face; I got a cursing for it. The gentleman said he would run his bayonet through me if I did that again.

A few negroes were still with me. I had hired them to gather my corn, and they had just started in with a load, when they met the Federals. The negroes had a yoke of oxen to the wagon and the soldiers made them take the oxen out and they drove them off with the other cattle, and the negro man returned to the house.

I was sitting on the steps seeing it all. He came up to me and said: "Missus, you ought not to have struck that man's horse; that's what made them take the oxen." I said I did not care; they had taken nearly all I had, and I would as soon die as live.

PLEADED IN VAIN

There was a young paroled soldier, a neighbor, and he went to their camp that evening and pleaded with them to give up the oxen, but the lieutenant, a very gallant gentleman, said they would not and sent me word to go to him and he would tell me what he thought of me. I did not go to find out.

At another time I was away from home a day or two, and when I returned, the first thing that I saw was the top of my corn crib torn off. I knew what that meant. The Federal soldiers had been there in my absence and taken nearly all my corn.

STOLE HUSBAND'S HORSE

One time my husband sent his horse home with a very sore back. I doctored him and fattened him. He was a fine riding horse. One day I was sitting at a window and saw two soldiers coming through the field. I went out the back hall door where I could see the horse in the horse lot. I was afraid they would take him. I stood there some time and did not see the Federals pass. I stepped back to the hall door and there they stood in the hall. They said: "What did you get up from the window for? Your husband is home and you went out to tell him to hide."

I replied: "He is not at home."

They said they know better, and that was what I went out for. It made me so angry I said: "I don't tell lies, and if you want to know what I went out for it was to see if you were going to take my horse."

They went to the horse lot and looked in his mouth and when they came in again they said: "You need not hide that horse tonight." I told him I was not going to hide him, but I knew they were going to take him, so when I got up next morning I went to look for him and he was gone. They did not take him out through the gate, but let the fence down at the back of the lot.

GOT OXEN AND HORSE BACK

The same paroled soldier that tried to get them to give up the oxen, followed them ten miles next morning and pleaded so hard they gave them up. Well, I sent for this young man and we went to the next house about a mile from my house where the wagon train had staid that night. There was a plantation of corn there, that the owner had ran off and left as soon as the Federals took Little Rock. The ground was frozen and I could hear the train going before we got there and, when we got there every one was gone, but the one who had my horse, and he was just starting. I rode up to him and said:

"That is my horse. What are you going to do with him? I want my horse."

I was determined to follow him to Little Rock if he did not give him up.

He eyed the young man with me for he had his gray uniform on. Once the fellow put his hand back on his gun, but he did not scare us. We stood there quite a while. I kept telling him to give up my horse, so at last he gave him to me, saying to the young man: "She's got a brudder or brudder-in-law that has put the devilment in her head."

That was my husband's brother, Captain J. M. Vance, that came with Steele's army. I went home with the horse and took a little nephew and went to Little Rock. I rode the horse. We did not overtake the wagon train until we got to the arsenal. I got a pass to go South, went home and got a little boy to go with me.

FINDING MONROE'S REGIMENT

We started to find Monroe's regiment. I heard it was at Arkadelphia. I rode that horse, for I was determined the Federals should not have him. We went a long way and heard the regiment was at Princeton, so we went there. I inquired in the town and they told me the regiment was camped at the edge of town. After two or three days the news came that the Federals were coming, and our boys hustled out. I told the boy that came with me we would meet the Federals, but he must not tell them which road our soldiers took.

Sure enough, we had not gone far until we met them. An officer asked us how far we had come. I told him. He then asked if any rebel troops were there. I told him "no." Then he wanted to know when they left and what road they took. I told him I did not know. He spoke very crossly, and said: "It is very strange, Madam, you don't know." Then he turned to the boy and spoke crossly to him, and he got scared and said they went down the Camden road. I left the horse with my husband and rode a sore-back pony that belonged to the negro man that my husband had with him.

A set of vagabonds sprung up as soon as the Federals took Little Rock. They went to General Steele and told a tale of woe about how they had been treated, and he let them form companies. They called themselves Home Guards. My husband and two of his men were on a scout and were slipped upon by those men and shot. He was killed and one of his men wounded and a boy who had taken them some papers was shot, while telling them not to shoot him, that he was no soldier, but they shot him and badly wounded him.

————————— ᵉᵍᵉᵉᵍᵉ —————————

CARING FOR SICK SOLDIERS IN GRANVILLE COUNTY, N. C.

During the war our women of Granville Co., N. C., being far from the front, pined for the opportunity of doing something for our sons, brothers and loved ones who were bravely defending their homes and firesides. So after consulting together they decided to ask the authorities at Richmond for one hundred or more sick or convalescent soldiers to nurse back to health. Their request was granted and the sick arrived from the hospitals, pale, weak,and wounded. They were met and warmly welcomed to homes and hearts. Some families took four, some two, others more as they had room.

How kindly and how proudly and tenderly they were ministered to by the gentle hands of our patriotic women can be imagined, and how the tired, suffering soldiers enjoyed the cool country and fresh milk and butter, the complete rest and quiet, was shown by their rapid restoration to health and strength.

All too soon, it seemed to us, they were called back, their furlough ended, and they returned for duty with renewed vigor and pleasant memories of a delightful furlough.

MRS. M. A. HARRIS

Henderson, N. C.

———————ଉଌ୍ଷ·ଈ·ଔଉ———————

MISS BARRINGTON'S BRAVERY
By Mrs. F. L. Sutton, of Fayetteville

There is a heroism,that seldom reaches the light of history, but it is nevertheless just as lofty, just as genuine, as that displayed at Thermopylae, Yorktown, the Alamo—the heroism of women during a great, fierce war.

A tithe has never been told of the deeds of daring, the brave defenses, the ministries of mercy, performed by the women of the South during the terrible war between the states. I say South because she is the land of my cradling, and her lot was mine during the long four years of cruel strife—a time when frequently it was a costly struggle even to exist. In those days women and little children lived indefinitely without visible means of support, sometimes not seeing a dollar for months, or if they had the means, in large portions of the country there was almost nothing to be had. Much of the time they subsisted upon the simple fruits that grew wild, cornbread, sorghum molasses and sassafras tea without sugar or cream.

Were there crops to be made, women made them; were fences to be built, women must build them. They raised houses, rolled logs, went to mill, not with two fat sleek horses for a team, but more likely the family cow and a big calf yoked together. It was women that killed hogs and beeves, and in the absence of these brutes, women shouldered guns and went hunting or fishing. In the absence of physicians (and there was a dearth of them for a long period), women practiced without leave or license, sometimes with greater success than some college men with diplomas to recommend them. But more pathetic still, it sometimes fell to woman's part not only to offer the final prayer in behalf of the dying and close the sightless eyes, but with her own hands, aided by other women to dig the grave, make the rude pine coffin, and after reading the burial service to fill the grave, mark the place with a simple board. then leave his body to nature and his soul to God.

But for a single deed of unsurpassed heroism, I recall a most thrilling incident in the life of a young lady, Miss Mat Barrington of north Arkansas. She lived with her aged mother a few miles from Fayetteville, which town was at this time occupied as a post by the Federal troops. A scouting party from the post had gone out into the country on the pitiless mission of harassing and plundering. At the home of Mrs. Barrington they swept everything in the smokehouse and emptied the larder. The last article was a bag of coffee ("Lincoln coffee," as it was known in those days). A broad-shouldered soldier seized upon this when the daughter raised complaint. She said: "I have stood by and watched you take all the rest without objecting, but the coffee my old mother needs above everything else, and I ask you to leave it." The soldier gave no heed to her request, but snatched up the bag and was making for the door, when she rushed for an iron poker and dealt him such a blow that he fell limp to the floor. As soon as he could recover himself he fled from the house leaving the coffee behind.

In a brief time the story of her deed reached the ears of friends in the remoter Dixie. The boys in gray at once voted that such a splendid triumph should not go unrewarded, and in due time there came to her a most magnificent saddle horse, with a tribute to her bravery.

The lady still lives, doubtless with her brown curls all silvered and wearing another name, but without the power or inclination to get away from the story of the bluecoat, the bag of coffee, the poker and the saddle horse.

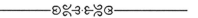

MISS McSWEENY AS A CONFEDERATE SPY, OF FORT SMITH
By J. M. Lucey

When the Federal general, Blunt, occupied Fort Smith late in 1863-4 and General W. L. Cabell retired from the city to Devil's Backbone, 18 miles distant, the intermediate territory became the raiding ground of both armies. A family named McSweeney lived near the public road, about half way between the two places. It was composed of a widow, her two daughters, Mattie and Mollie, aged about 18 and 12, respectively, and a son, Peter, aged about 20. The last named was in Cabell's brigade. Miss Mattie visited Fort Smith twice a week at irregular intervals, according as her escort, a young Federal lieutenant, could arrange for an absence. She was under suspicion at Blunt's headquarters, but confidence was placed in the detective powers of the lieutenant.

SOMETHING ON HIS MIND

One instance of her tact will be narrated out of several. On this occasion there seemed to be something on the lieutenant's mind which he was anxious to get off. There was two things on Miss Mattie's mind, tin cups and frying pans. News had been brought to her from Cabell's camp that tin cups and frying pans were badly needed. The gold that had been concealed for months in soldiers' belts was brought forth, so that there might be no delay on the score of money.

On this trip Miss Mattie stopped at the home of the writer's father, where his sisters and other ladies quickly arranged to make the purchases, as it would not do for Miss Mattie to buy the articles. In a few hours everything was secured and deftly fastened to her underclothing. Miss Mattie had made a special request that a negro driver would take her home, the lieutenant riding on horseback as an escort until the pickets were passed. What was the horror of all concerned when the buggy was driven up by the lieutenant!

Could it mean that a discovery was made? Captured as a spy would mean death to her and imprisonment to all concerned.

THE OFFICER HOODWINKED

A hasty council of war was held by the ladies and they came to the conclusion that there was nothing to it. One of the ladies went to hold the horse and the another induced the officer to enter the house for a lemonade, while the others were transferring the tin cups and frying pans to the other side from where he would ride. How the young lady got well fixed in the buggy before the officer came out, how they passed the time so that there would be no jingling and how her little sister effected a ruse by which Miss Mattie was enabled to make a safe landing are all matters of local history.

SEARCHING REFUGEES

Another kind of heroism was brought into existence when it became necessary in the eyes of the Federal commander to send the wives of Confederate soldiers or sympathizers beyond the lines. An officer would come to the house with an old negro woman. The trunks, traveling bags and even the clothing worn were to be searched for contraband goods. The main point of the lady friends of the refugees was to cajole the officer, mollycoddle him, and get the negro woman drunk. The residence of the Miller family, one of whom, Miss Adelaide, married Wm. M. Fishback, governor of the state at one time, was a favorite place of departure. The ladies would never give out the secrets of those occasions, and it was not for many years safe to do so, but it is known that midst the sadness and sorrows of farewells there were interesting events.

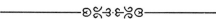

A SKETCH OF MRS. SALLIE WALLACE RUTHERFORD
By Mrs. Emilise Dowd, of Fort Smith

Sallie Wallace, daughter of Dr. Wallace and Jane Perry Butler, was born at Greenville, S. C., in 1837, and moved to Ft. Gibson, I. T., then a frontier post near Fort Smith, Ark., in 1849, when her father was appointed by Pres. Taylor agent for the Cherokee Indians.

Upon the death of Dr. Butler, Mrs. Butler moved to Fayetteville, Ark., in order that her children might have the educational advantages for which, even at that time, Fayetteville was justly famous; and there in 1854, Sallie Wallace was married to Robt. B. Rutherford of Fort Smith, who had just graduated from The University school, together with many others who afterward achieved distinction in the service of their State.

Mr. and Mrs. Rutherford moved to Lewisville, Ark., just prior to the Civil war, and when the men were called to the defense of their State and Southland. Mrs. Rutherford, like most Southern women, was left to provide and care for her family, and with it all to give abundantly of her little to a hungry or distressed Confederate soldier.

Her cheerful self reliance and wonderful strength of character, inherited from her Scotch and English ancestry, through the New England mother and Cavalier father, stood her in good hand now during these dark and perilous times and the yet darker ones of the Reconstruction period.

Mrs. Rutherford has always felt the deepest interest in all that affects her adopted State and no woman in its borders enjoys to a higher degree the love and respect of all who know her. She is not only the possessor of a happy and optimistic nature, but of a rare and practical intellect, which has made her for years an important factor in church and philanthropic enterprizes in Fort Smith and particularly is she always interested in matters concerning the South.

In her old age she remains a true daughter of the Old South, and to quote her own words is "Unreconstructed still." She finds much pleasure in recalling the days of 1861-65 at Fort Smith, when the sewing circle and daily visits to the temporary hospitals took up all her time.

Mrs. Beard, mother of Willie Beard, a Confederate Soldier, was frequently her companion and is very happily remembered by the old soldiers. Mrs. Sophy Kannady, Mrs. J. K. McKensie, the Gookan girls, and many others were among those who bore a distinguished part in passing events.

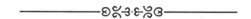

JEFFERSON DAVIS' SUGGESTED INSCRIPTION FOR MONUMENT TO WOMEN OF CONFEDERACY

(This inscription is practically Jefferson Davis' dedication of his "Rise and Fall of the Confederate Government," but somewhat altered.)

TO THE WOMEN OF THE SOUTHERN CONFEDERACY

Whose loving ministrations nursed
the wounded to health,
And soothed the last hours of the dying;
Whose unselfish labors
Supplied the wants of their defenders in the field.

Whose unwavering faith in our cause
Showed ever a guiding star,
Through the perils and disasters of war;
Whose sublime fortitude
Sustained them under every privation and all suffering;
Whose floral offerings
Are yearly laid upon the graves of those
Whom they still honor and love; and
Whose patriotism
Will teach their children
To emulate tho deeds of their Confederate sires,
But who with a modesty, excelled only by their worth
Have ever discouraged
This tribute to their noble virtues.

———————ᴈ⧢ᴈ·ᴈ-⧢ᴈ———————

A SKETCH OF MRS. SOPHIA KANNADY, A HEROINE OF FORT SMITH
By W. J. Weaver, of Fort Smith

Mrs. Sophia Kanady was born in Fort Gibson, Indian Territory, in 1826. She was the daughter of Aaron and Rebecca Barling, who came to Fort Smith when this post was established by Col. Long in 1817, but who removed to Fort Gibson when that post was established by the government several years afterward. When she was two years old her parents returned to Arkansas, and her father purchased a farm about eight miles east of Fort Smith. This farm is still in possession of the Barling family. Not far from the home and upon the road leading to Little Rock was, and is yet, a spring of strong sulphur water. The Barling home was a favorite stopping place for travelers in the ante-bellum days and in summer time it was often a resort for people who wished to spend a few weeks in the invigorating air of the country. Young beaux and their sweethearts would often ride from the town to Barling's Spring on Sunday afternoons or at such times as might suit their convenience and pleasure. The doors of the old fashioned country home were always open, and visitors were always sure of a hearty welcome from its inmates.

It may not be uninteresting to note an incident that occurred in the early life of Miss Barling, while she was acquiring an education. There were no public schools in Arkansas in those days. The private schools were few and far between, and in them were taught only the elementary branches of instruction. Miss Barling's parents were determined on giving her more of an education than the limited facilities of the country afforded, and after she had acquired about all there was to be obtained in Fort Smith, determined upon sending her to a school taught by Professor Maro for young ladies, in St. Louis. On her trip to what is now the great metropolis of the Southwest, but which was then a comparatively small town, she rode from Fort Smith to Neosho, Mo., on horseback. From there she rode the remainder of the way in a buggy, and upon arriving in St. Louis entered the school and remained there 18 months. This was in 1839.

Returning home after the finishing touches had been placed upon her scholastic life, she remained under the parental roof until 1847 when she was married to Jerre R. Kannady, the marriage ceremony being conducted by Rev. C. C. Townsend, the first clergyman of the Episcopal church that ever officiated in Fort Smith. Mr.

Kannady was a native of Pennsylvania and came to this country in 1835.

From the date of their marriage until the blighting hand of Northern aggression fell upon the Southern states, Mr. and Mrs. Kannady lived a life of contentment and happiness. Mr. Kannady opened a blacksmith and wagon shop, to which was afterwards added a grist mill and a sawmill. Business prospered and money came rapidly, but it never remained long in the hands of this worthy and lovable couple — it went really faster than it came for their doors were ever open and their table ever free to all who called. They kept "open house" to all from the time they moved into their one-story log house with its big chimney at one end and its wide hallway from front to rear until after the close of the war. They had no children of their own, but they cared for the children of others, for relatives less fortunate than themselves in the accumulation of this world's goods, and for others who were not relatives hundreds of whom were the recipients of their benevolence and charity. Mr. Kannady passed away April 25, 1882, mourned by everybody who knew him, and since that time his widow has lived a quiet life, surrounded by relatives and friends, her declining years sweetened by the kind attentions of those who knew her in the olden times — the times upon which her tenderest memories dwell.

The most strenuous (to us a popular nowaday's phrase) period of Mrs. Kannady's life was doubtless embraced in the four years of the war for Southern independence. She was busy every moment of that time, discharging not only the duties of her home life but working night and day for the comfort of the Confederate soldier. Perhaps a few of the most stirring scenes through which she passed can best be given in her own words, as related to the writer.

"The war was a trying time for all, women as well as men. Of course while the men had hardships and dangers of the battlefield and camp-life to confront, the women had no less laborious and trying tasks to perform. They had to care for the sick and aged, the destitute women and children whose husbands and fathers were in the field, and had to do much in taking care of the sick and wounded soldiers, and O, how much suffering they witnessed.

"The first sign we had of real war" says Mrs Kannady "was when the State troops came up from Little Rock to capture Fort Smith, then under command of Capt. Sturgis. They came on boats. At Van Buren they divided, some of them proceeding upon the boats and the others marching into town over the road leading from Van Buren to Fort Smith. The regular troops were in the garrison. Capt. Sturgis was notified by the telegraph operator at Van Buren of the approach of the State forces, and caused the 'long roll' to be sounded. That was the first time I had ever heard it. We had working for us a couple of men who had formerly been in the regular army and they became very much excited. One of them rushed out of the house and looked up and down Garrison Avenue to see what was coming. 'Ah, Mrs. Kannady' said he, 'that means danger.' But these men were not the only people in the town who were excited. We were all excited, for we did not know but that a battle would take place right at our own doors. But no danger resulted from the approach of the

State troops, for Sturgis left the town that night, going out the Texas road and on to Fort Washita.

"Another time we had a bad scare, or a Stampede, as we called it, was one night when a number of "Pins" or Federal Indians crossed the river. We were greatly alarmed, for there were but few Confederate troops here at the time. Officers galloped about the streets shouting that the "Pins" were ravaging the country around the town and calling upon the men to arm themselves and turn out. The women and children were frantically urged to go into the garrison. All the buildings in the garrison were at that time filled with sick and wounded soldiers, which added to the distress and confusion, as we did not know but what they would all be murdered. The "Pins" however, did no further harm than to burn George Minmire's house about three miles north of town.

"As soon as the war began the ladies of the town organized sewing societies to make clothing for the soldiers. We met at first in the Methodist Church. We would work all day long, making coats, jackets, pants, tents, wagon sheets, haversacks and such things, and at night we would knit socks. I was a cutter, and cut hundreds and hundreds of suits for soldiers and officers. We would also scrape lint and make bandages for the wounded. Later on we had to give up the church for use as a hospital, and then we met in different houses, or did the sewing in our own homes. Many of the women worked in their homes at making cartridges. Later in the war the work became more trying and the scenes were awful. Sick men from the surrounding armies and wounded men from the battlefields were brought in. The old red mill near the head of Garrison

Avenue, lately torn down, was used as a hospital, so was Bright's store, Sutton's store on the corner of Garrison Avenue and Second Street, the Methodist and Presbyterian Churches, and in fact all the vacant houses in the town were used to shelter the sick and wounded. All the quarters in the garrison also contained sick and wounded soldiers. Besides this, many families in town took sick and wounded men into their homes and cared for them until they either got well or died. The Episcopal and Catholic Churches were not used as hospitals. Much of our time then was taken up in preparing food for the hospitals and in taking care of the sick and wounded. We would go to the hospitals and sometimes wash and dress the patients and care for their wounds. This was awful work, and sometimes it would keep us in the hospital all day. Every empty house in the town was filled with the wounded after the battle of Oak Hill. Jerre and I kept open house all this time, treating officers, privates and refugees all alike. One day shortly after the battle of Oak Hill we fed forty people. I remember that four Texas soldiers came one day and told me they wanted something to eat. Dinner was over and I told them I did not believe I had anything for them, but I got them up a dinner and they ate heartily. When they got ready to leave they laid five dollars in gold upon the table. I refused to take it. They insisted, and told me that had they known I would take no pay for the meal they would not have come. I did not take it, however, and told them that I never charged anybody for a meal.

"Those were awful times too, after the battles of Elk Horn and Prairie Grove. Generals McCulloch and McIntosh were killed at Elk Horn, and General Steen was killed at Prairie Grove. General McCulloch's body was brought to Fort Smith and then sent to Texas. Generals McIntosh and Steen were buried here in what is now the National Cemetery.

"I believe the greatest danger I was in during the war, was when Mr. Kannady and I were captured by Captain Hart and his gang of Federal bushwhackers as we were returning from Texas. This was in January, 1863. We had gone to Texas earlier in the year, and on our way home we were captured near Big Creek, about twenty miles from Fort Smith. On the day before, Hart and his gang killed Col. DeRosey Carrol and Mr. Sam Richardson. It was raining very hard at the time and was very cold. Hart lifted me off of my horse. He was a fine looking man, and while he robbed us of our team, provisions and everything else we had, he did not cause me to be searched, nor did he take my horse. There was a house near the place where we were captured, and as it was raining hard I wanted to go to it. Hart told me I might go, but when I requested that Jerre might go with me, he said no. After that I would not leave Jerre's side, for from the way they acted and from what they said I was satisfied they intended to kill him. Some of Hart's men said they were going to hang Jerre, and I am certain they would have done so, had it not been for a negro who interceded for his life. I believe he would have hung both of us but for this negro. This negro, by the way, had been at the battle of Oak Hill, where he was wounded. I had in my pocket a revolver in which there were two loads, and I intended, if Jerre had been hung, to kill Hart and then kill myself. Jerre recognized several of the men in Hart's gang. They lived in the Vache Gras country, and before he left for Texas Jerre had supplied their families with meal and bacon to keep them from starving while their husbands were bush-whacking. The man who boasted to the negro that 'Jerre Kannady would never see Fort Smith again' was a man to whom Mr. Kannady had, some time before, issued provisions. This shows what kind of people they were.

"After Hart had decided not to hang my husband he placed us in a house belonging to a man named Coffey, who lived about five miles from Big Creek, where we were kept from Tuesday until the following Friday. Several Confederate soldiers whom Hart had captured were there at the same time. Hart did not harm these men, but when he went away put them upon parole. Some time during the last night we stayed at Coffey's somebody came to the house and told Jerre that he had better get away from there as soon as he could, and the next morning we left. Jerre hired two ponies, and these, with my horse and the horse of the faithful negro, got us back to Fort Smith. There were ten inches of snow on the ground when we started. A few days after this, Hart was captured at Smedley's mill and brought to Fort Smith, where he was tried, convicted and hanged.

"Jerre was very busy with his mills and blacksmith shop for a long time after the war began. Among the things he made were one thousand knives for Stand Watie's Cherokee Brigade. These knives were made of large files and had wooden handles. I have one of them now. He also made about two thousand powder horns, and I don't know how many drinking cups. The cups were made of horns sawed into proper size, with wooden bottoms. He also made a great many pipes, and there is no telling what he did make. There was a good supply of iron in the shop and the mills were stocked with looms, spinning wheels, and other articles which had been made there when the Federals came in, all of which the Federals seized.

"When the Federals came, September 1, 1863, we went to Texas, leaving the night before Cloud's regiment arrived. We bought a home in Bonham. I went nearly all over Texas while we lived there. Mr. Kannady was appointed by the government to establish mills and blacksmith shops for the Confederate government, and whenever he went off on one of his trips I went with him. We came back to Fort Smith in 1865."

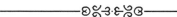

CAPTAIN SALLY TOMPKINS

Southern women have cared little for public honors nor have they courted masculine titles. But a recent number of the Richmond Times-Dispatch recalls the pleasant bit of history that in the case of Miss Sallie Tompkins a remarkable honor was deservedly conferred upon a worthy Virginia girl by the Confederate authorities.

While yet a very young woman Miss Tompkins used her ample means to establish in Richmond a private hospital for Confederate soldiers. She not only provided for its support at her own expense, but devoted her time to the work of nursing the patients.

The wounded were brought into the city by the hundreds and there was hardly a private house without its quota of sick and wounded. Quite a number of private hospitals were established but, unlike Miss Tompkins' splendid institution, charges were made by some of them for services rendered. In course of time abuses grew with the system, and General Lee ordered that they all be closed—all except the hospital of Miss Tompkins. This was recognized as too helpful to the Confederate cause to be abolished.

In order to preserve it, it had to be brought under government control, and to do this General Lee ordered a commission as captain in the Confederate army to be issued to Miss Sallie Tompkins. Though a government hospital from that time on, Captain Tompkins conducted it as before, paying its expenses out of her private purse.

The veterans are proud of her record, and a movement is now on foot among them to place Captain Tompkins in a position of independence as long as she lives.

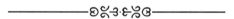

A SKETCH OF MRS. W. L. CABELL, OF FORT SMITH
By Her Husband, Lieutenant-General W. L. Cabell

Rev. J. M. Lucey:—

I have the honor to acknowledge receipt of your truly kind letter. It makes me feel, in my old age, that my sainted wife and myself still have friends who remember them in their young days, and I will try and comply with your request.

Mrs. Harriette Amanda Cabell was Miss Harriette Amanda Rector, daughter of Major Elias and Catherine Rector, of Fort Smith, Arkansas. Col. Rector was U. S.

Indian agent and subsequently U. S. Marshall. She was born the 3rd of June, 1837, and when a babe was given the name of "Shingo" by the Old Head Chief of the Osage Indians, Claremore. She was always called by that name until the day of her death. She was educated early at her old home school and graduated at the Sacred Heart Academy, at St. Louis, Mo. She was a great favorite with her classmates as well as with all who knew her, being noted for her great wit, and sweet, pretty manners. She was reigning belle of Arkansas and had many admirers, before her marriage to Lieutenant William L. Cabell, of the 7th Regiment United States Infantry, July 22, 1856. Soon after their marriage, Lieutenant Cabell carried his bride to Fort Gibson, in the Cherokee Nation, Indian Territory, and lived at different forts on the frontier until the war between the States, when she went to Virginia, in April 1861, with her husband.

She blessed her husband with seven children, two dying as infants. Four sons and one daughter grew to womanhood and manhood. Three sons and one daughter now live to bless the memory of their sainted mother.

Mrs. Shingo Cabell was one of the sweetest and most intellectual women of the South. She was a woman of great common sense and of remarkable firmness of character, with a heart full of love and affection. She was above all things a true Southern woman, in fact one of the queens of the South, and so proud of the Confederacy, and the Confederate soldier, that she never failed to administer to the wounded and comfort the dying. She would not enter in any social gatherings during the war, but devoted her time and that of her servants to preparing lint bandages, knitting socks and sending them to the soldiers.

At one time when I was a prisoner of war, General Magruder gave a ball in Washington, Hempstead County, Arkansas, and sent a special invitation to Mrs. Cabell to attend. She wrote him a very polite note declining, stating that he had better look after the comfort of nearly two hundred badly wounded soldiers of Cabell's Brigade and take the money to be expended at the ball and buy condiments and other necessaries for the comforts of the wounded and dying; that she would devote all her time to the sick and wounded soldier until her husband returned, if it was to the day of her death.

Those were the sentiments that made her beloved by the Confederate soldier. She was a woman of great firmness, as brave as a lion, and at the same time as gentle as a lamb. No one knew her but to love her. She belonged to a number of charitable associations and was always doing good in her home in Arkansas and her home in Texas. So much was she beloved by the Arkansas soldiers that they would cheer her on all public occasions whenever she made her appearance.

She died on the 16th of April, 1887, while on a visit to her friends and relatives in Arkansas. She was brought back and buried in the cemetery in Dallas, Texas, in the presence of two-thirds of the citizens of Dallas. She was laid gently in her tomb covered with flowers. Her children have erected a monument over the grave and on one side is engraved in beautiful letters the name "Shingo Cabell."

Your friend,
W. L. CABELL

DID IT HERSELF

An incident was related to the writer in 1863 at Fort Smith, where Mrs. Cabell had her home, which illustrates her strength of character and her ready wit. General Cabell was reported to be very sick at Clarksville, Ark. Some ladies went to her one day and said: "Oh, Mrs. Cabell, we have heard some awful things and we think we ought to tell you. General Cabell is very sick in the Clarksville hospital and what do you think, several young ladies who were waiting on him fell in love with him. The consequences may be terrible." Mrs. Cabell replied: "Is that all, ladies? Why I cannot see how those young ladies could have done otherwise than fall in love with General Cabell, I did it myself."

J. M. L.

The day after her marriage at Fort Smith, July 22, 1856, Mrs. Cabell yielded to urgent solicitation and had her picture taken. It was a daguerreotype, and this is the only instance when she would consent to have any form of picture taken. When General Cabell was captured, 1864, and carried as a prisoner to Johnson Island, a small photo was made from the old daguerreotype and sent to him. It reached him safely and was the most cherished thing that he had in his prison life. He was reluctant, even now, to part with it for a few days, but consented to allow it to be used for the cut that appears in this book, so that the face of his beloved wife might have a place among the loved and loving Arkansas Daughters of the Confederacy.

Mrs. Katie Cabell Muse, only daughter of General and Mrs. Cabell, has been a prominent figure in all the women's movements for the preservation of the glories of the Confederacy. In 1877, she was elected National President of the U. D. C. organization at Baltimore, Md., and in 1898, at Hot Springs, Ark., she was re-elected by acclamation.

———————ⓈⓈⒾⒺⓎⒼⒶ———————

SKETCH OF JUDGE ROGERS AND FAMILY, OF FORT SMITH

John Henry Rogers, soldier, lawyer, Congressman, and jurist, was born on a plantation near Roxobel, Bertie County, N. C., October 9, 1845, the third child of Absalom and Harriet Rogers, and grandson of William Rogers, a farmer and mechanic, who lived and reared a family of twelve children in Pitt County, N. C. His father was a wealthy planter before the war, but, being deprived of his slaves and everything but his land, was reduced to poverty by that disaster.

In March, 1862, he was mustered into the Ninth Regiment, Mississippi Infantry, at Canton, Miss., as a private. In the battle of Munfordville (Green River), Ky., he was wounded while charging the enemy's breastworks. He was subsequently in the battles of Murfreesboro (Stone River), Tenn., Chickamauga, Ga., Mission Ridge, near Chattanooga, Tenn., and Resaca, Ga. He was in the engagements, before Atlanta, July 26 and 28, 1864, and was wounded at Jonesboro, Ga., in September, 1864. He fought at Franklin, Tenn., November 30, 1864, and at Nashville, Tenn., December 15, 1864. In April, 1865, although but nineteen years of age, he was promoted by special order of General

Johnston to rank of first lieutenant, and he commanded Company F of the Ninth Mississippi Regiment until the capitulation of Johnston's army.

His address before the general reunion of United Confederate Veterans at New Orleans, May, 1903, is considered the best one ever given before that body. Several thousand copies were distributed.

Judge Rogers was married October 9, 1873, to Mary Gray, only daughter of Dr. Theodore Dunlap and Elizabeth Gray, of Danville, Ky. Four sons and one daughter are living, their first child, Theodora, having died at the age of two years. Miss Bessie Rogers was married October 24, 1905, to Mr. Ray Meredith Johnston, of Fort Smith, Ark. Both mother and daughter have taken great interest in all that relates to the Lost Cause, and are entitled to very much consideration by the old veterans. Modesty has prevented them from giving a sketch of their many good acts.

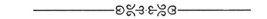

HUSBAND AND FIVE BROTHERS IN THE WAR
By Mrs. Mahaley Pollard, of Gray

My husband and five brothers joined the Confederate army from my old home in Alabama and I was left with six small children to support My husband was severely wounded at Shiloh, where so many Arkansas soldiers lost their lives. My husband, B. M. Pollard joined Company D., Twenty-second Alabama regiment in 1861, and surrendered at Raliegh, N. C., in 1865. He was in the battles of Shiloh, Vicksburg, Chickamauga,

Stone Mountain, Murfreesboro, and others, almost all the time under General Joe Johnston. He died five years after the close of the war. I am now 69 years old and a widow for 38 years. In 1881 we moved to Woodruff County, Arkansas.

ROUGH TIMES DURING THE WAR

I had a hard time in the war period, as the Northern soldiers took everything that I had or destroyed what they could not carry off. They emptied my feather bed and pillows and killed my cows and hogs, leaving me nothing. How little those rough soldiers thought of the hardships they were inflicting upon women and children. If they imagined such cruel privations as they generally forced upon Southern women would have the effect of discouraging them from working in the aid of the Confederacy, they were sadly mistaken. Our soldiers acted bravely on the field of battle and we women tried to be worthy of them.

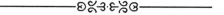

FEDERAL RAIDERS AND THEIR CRUELTIES
By Mrs. J. B. Crump, of Harrison

The border of north Arkansas was during the war a theater of tragedy, The Union men, as they were called, were in the minority, and left their homes to "go back and forth," and thereby inaugurate a system of warfare against the defenseless families whose men folks were enlisted on the other side.

Four decades have passed since, those times of peril, and criticisms are unnecessary on the conduct of those who, from principle or provocation, refused to espouse the cause of the Confederacy.

But with the purpose unbiased save by love for our native heath, I have gathered from hills and valleys authentic records of those who shared in our common dangers, trials and privations.

To preserve these acts of heroism is to cultivate a noble sentiment that idealizes the principle and love of the cause that prompted those acts and to save from oblivion (for the benefit of future generations) unimpeachable facts as yet untouched by history.

'Twas in the fall of '63, directly after the surrender of the Confederate forces in Little Rock, Ark., when Price had gone South, that Crooked Creek was a temporary rendezvous for a band of lawless refugees.

DEFENSELESS HOME ATTACKED

Under the cover of night a party attacked the defenseless home of John Bailey, who was infirm with age.

With bitter curses and angry commands they aroused the sleeping family, consisting of Mr. Bailey, his delicate wife and only daughter, and demanded admission.

The sons of the family (all brave soldiers in the Confederate army) had their clothes packed in saddlebags ready to follow Price at their first opportunity, and the Mother and sister well knew that access to their apartments meant the loss of clothing for the rebels.

"Make a light or we'll make one for you," blurted out a gruff voice from the front piazza.

"Ring the bell, mother," whispered the daughter, "as if the boys are in hearing, while I engage the attention of those in front of the house."

The fearless mother rang the bell until the very night air seemed full of warning to the startled intruders.

"Shut up your infernal ringing there; I'll not be thwarted by an old woman," said the leader of this ruffian band and, seizing the frail little mother, he threw her full length in the yard below, where she lay as if lifeless.

The daughter, who had adroitly been "killing time," by pretending to take from the candle molds a candle with which to furnish a light, heard her mother shriek, saw the atrocious act, saw her mother apparently dead from his cruelty, then unhesitatingly confronted the would-be assassin with a desperation born of despair.

"You scoundrel! See, you have killed my mother!" and scarcely were the words spoken when, she rushed forward to the edge of the piazza. where the outlaw was standing, and dealt him a blow across the eyes with the unemptied candle molds that sent him staggering backward. Wildly clutching at the railing he went down to the ground, to, be carried away by his comrades from the scene of action, a "wiser if not a better man."

Mrs. Bailey suffered much from her fall, but her life was spared to see her four sons, "bronzed and battle scarred," return home when war and its strife were over.

And in offering this simple tribute to womanly courage we feel assured that duty had no more ardent votaries or the "lost cause" more devoted champions than these two brave women.

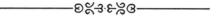

TWO BRAVE WOMEN
By Mrs. J. B. Crump, of Harrison

There are heroines on our north Arkansas border without laurels on their brows, and martyrs "in whose hands are no palms" that went through physical hardships, isolation and distress and to whom our late war is as a terrible dream.

The smoke from the charred ruins of their only earthly habitations—the terror-stricken faces of the homeless, starving children, are singularly confused now—but the time was when these same privations whetted the edge of their mental natures, until their ingenuity and invention were almost unsurpassed.

Hundreds of miles from a railroad or telegraph, and menaced by a lawlessness that lived by terrorism to women and children, these heroines were made self-reliant through danger and imbued with a courage rarely equaled.

WOMEN AND CHILDREN MADE CROPS

The cultivation of land, or a scanty living from the hills, and valleys of this border, was made through much difficulty by women and children. It was in the spring and summer of '64 that Mrs. Parker, now living in Boone County, Ark., made with the assistance of her little boy, a good corn crop for that day and time. The yoke of steers with which Mrs. Parker trudged early and late, were taken from her time and again, but through persistent appeals to the Federal officers she was allowed to keep them until her corn was "laid by."

After days of watching and working the crop was gathered and stored away in a pen (Mrs. Parker had made it herself of rails in the woods.)

But as the scarcity of food demanded a more thorough investigation on the part of the enemy, this noble woman dug with her own hands a hole in which she placed a hogshead that held twelve bushels of corn.

SAVED ALL HER CORN

From the pen in the woods she carried the corn, shelled it and filled the hogshead, which she covered so dextrously with dirt and leaves that even she had some difficulty in finding her buried treasure.

In spite of the stories circulated by a traitorous tenant who had shared her bread and partaken of her kindness, Mrs. Parker kept the corn unmolested until Confederates came home "in the gloom of defeat."

And during the spring peace was made. Small allowances from the underground hogshead were issued to the starving neighbors by this kind-hearted woman.

Jealously did she guard this "trust fund" and not a grain was squandered or lost, but went as a blessing to succor the perishing at her door.

PRIVATIONS BORNE WITH A SMILE
By Mrs. DeFontaine

"The boys at the front were the first consideration. After their wants were supplied, only what was left could be utilized by those at home. To do without was part of a Southern woman's religion.

"One velvet jacket came out triumphant at the end of the war, having done heroic duty for five girls of the family on all festive occasions.

"If there were two girls in the family, we went out singly, in order that the same dress might do double duty. We borrowed, loaned, patched, lengthened, shortened, turned and twisted our garments until there was nothing left of them.

"A Richmond belle at a party, usually the gayest of the gay, was asked why she was not dancing. 'Dancing,' she said, 'Good heavens, I am only too thankful that I can, breathe. I don't even dare to laugh for fear I should burst this girl's dress to pieces and it is all she has.'

"In the absence of men, the women undertook their duties, and many a fine crop was planted and harvested by them.

"Two Georgia women did what no other woman in the world has been credited with—cleaned out a well. and did it well."

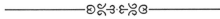

HUSBAND KILLED AT SHILOH
By Mrs. Anna Mitchell, of Havana

My husband and oldest brother joined the Tenth Arkansas Regiment near Quitman. C. R. Merrick was colonel and Witt (afterward colonel) and W. W. Martin of Conway were captains. The regiment camped near home two or three weeks and we felt so proud of them. We made our men red shirts, trimmed with black, and with white thread worked in "Quitman Rifles." We covered their canteens the same way. I remembered covering one for Bob Bertrand of Little Rock.

PROMISED TO "WHIP THE YANKEES"

Our boys promised us that they would whip the Yankees right away and then come home and we would all have a fine time. We believed every word they said, and, loath as we were to give them up, we spoke our farewells bravely and waved in joy our little flags. We waited many a long day for their return!

WOMEN PLOWING

My father had a large family, and the only one able to work, my oldest brother, had joined the army. We had a hard time to keep body and soul together. The women plowed the field and planted and cultivated the corn. Some women had to walk five miles to a mill to get meal for their sack of corn, and frequently there was no meal, nothing but bran, which they cooked and ate.

It was a common sight on the road to the mill to see two women on either side of a yearling calf that was harnessed to the front or rear part of a wagon, with a small load of corn or wheat. Each woman held a line from the head of the yearling, and the work of the day was to induce the yearling to walk forward and not backward.

SPINNING AND WEAVING

Mother and myself never knew one day what we would have to eat or wear the next. Spinning and weaving constantly was one part of our work. When our homes began to look comfortable, the Federal raiders would come and take horses, food and clothing. We had then to begin all things over again.

My husband was killed at the battle of Shiloh, and the whole work of rearing the family fell upon me. Many times I grieved that I could not give them something good to eat, but it was only when they began to grow into manhood that their life became what I wished it to be. My three sons are now living, one a doctor, another a lawyer and another a merchant.

EXTRAVAGANCE AND PRIDE OF THE YOUNG

The present generation thinks that the old folks are too economical in their ways. If they had gone through the war times they would not be so extravagant. Nor would they be working to place themselves above one another. In the old times all were on an equality. Those that never had to work had to learn very soon or do without much clothing. Then they were glad to get their poor neighbors to show them how to spin thread and weave cloth to make their dresses, and when they were made those fine ladies were just as proud of them as if they had the finest silk.

PROUD OF BEING A SOUTHERN GIRL

In the war times we were proud of being Southern girls. We gloried in the name and felt greater pride in it than in glittering wealth or fame. Hurrah for the home-spun dresses that our Southern women wore! These goods were really nice, so that you could not always tell them from store goods, though we did not have ribbons and fringes to hide defects. My children, when they see this poor writing, may feel ashamed of their old mother's inability as a writer, but it will be the first time in their lives that they did not love what the old lady did.

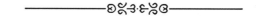

WEAVING JEANS FOR THE CONFEDERATES
By Mrs. M. C. Livingston, of Hope

I am now over 78 years old and am blessed with my second eyesight for the past three years, not needing glasses. When my husband enlisted in the Confederate army I was left with five children. My oldest child was 10 years old and the youngest six weeks. We were living upon a farm and now there was no one to make a crop for me. I hired the wheat sowed, raised my own meat and bought corn. Two of my children learned to card and spin, and we gave many a yard of cloth for a bushel of corn.

WEAVING JEANS FOR CONFEDERATES

The soldiers needed clothing and the quartermasters would encourage the women to weave jeans and sell it to the government. In this way I managed to have a little money all the time. A Mr. Murphy used to tan leather and make our shoes, for which we would pay in jeans.

Some men in Louisiana made salt there and peddled it out in Arkansas at the rate of $10 a bushel. I was able to buy some every trip they made to my house.

FEDERAL RAIDERS

It was a lonely time for me, with only my children for companions. How scared I was when the Federal raiders came the first time! They did not treat me as badly as they did several of my neighbors. They killed some of my cattle and took all my meat except a few middlings, having got all my honey, butter, eggs, and all the chickens that they could catch.

My husband was not a strong man, and was frequently in the hospital. I wrote to him to keep all the money that he had to buy things for himself, and that I would take care of the family. For six months I did not hear from him, and I was in a fearful state of mind.

For two years I had no chance to attend a prayer meeting or go to church. I read my Bible and prayed the good Lord to forgive me if I was not serving him as I ought. There was no school, and I taught my children the common branches of an education. When my husband came home there was joy in the house. I have now been a widow for 21 years. The good Lord has blessed me and has made me unspeakably happy in so many ways that I am now contented and happy and just waiting for Him to call me home.

GENERAL FORREST'S TRIBUTE

There is a story told by General Forrest which shows his opinion of the pluck and devotion of the Southern women. He was drawing up his men in line of battle one day, and it was evident that a sharp encounter was about to take place. Some ladies ran from a house which happened to stand just in front of his line, and asked him anxiously: "What shall we do, General, what shall we do?" Strong in his faith that they only wished to help in some way, he replied, "I really don't see that you can do much, except to stand on stumps, wave your bonnets and shout, 'Hurrah, Boys.'"

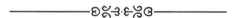

HOSPITAL WORK OF JUDGE JAMES GREEN AND WIFE
By Their Son, B. W. Green, of Little Rock

In the early spring of 1863, my parents were living in North Georgia near Dalton. They sold their plantation and began an overland journey with their negroes to Arkansas, where they owned a cotton plantation in Hempstead County. Before the War Between the States they had sent a part of their negroes in charge of two sons, to this State and they wished to unite their forces on this cotton plantation, but the movement of General Grant's army south from Memphis, made the risk of crossing the Mississippi river too great. My father, Judge James Green, was too old to enter the Confederate army but his heart was in the work, he having furnished six sons for the service and he therefore determined to offer his service to the Confederate States in hospital work. His services were accepted and he was assigned to duty at Tunnel Hill, Georgia, as superintendent of the hospital. My mother had been accustomed to the ease and comfort which wealth affords, but seeing the great need for skillful nursing in the hospital, she determined to undertake the post of Matron under my father. She gave herself up wholly to this duty day and night to the end of the war. When Sherman advanced against Dalton the hospital was removed to South Georgia, and when Hood advanced into Tennessee the hospital was sent to Columbus, Mississippi. After the evacuation of Tennesee, the army being sent to North Carolina, the hospital was sent to Forsythe, Georgia, and remained there until the end of the war. My mother did not spare herself when there was suffering and sick soldiers to be nursed; she went into the smallpox wards and where there were other contagious diseases without fear and with her own hands ministered to their wants. After one of our great battles had been fought there was a stream of wounded men who were sent from the front and cared for in the hospital by my parents. They had six boys in the line of gray, one in the Trans-Mississippi department, four in the army of Tennessee, and one in Virginia, and in most every battle fought from Texas to Virginia one of her boys was in the line of battle. This constant anxiety of mind and tax upon her physical strength and sympathy finally broke down her superb constitution and she never fully regained her health; yet she lived to be seventy-six years old, dying in the city of Hope, Arkansas, some years after the war ended. My father was treasurer of Hempstead County at the time of his death, which occurred before that of my mother. Their joint service in hospital work was a labor of love, for they served free of charge to the Confederate States. Nothing was too hard for them to undertake in order to save the lives of our soldier boys committed to their care. While hundreds were nursed back to life and health by their untiring efforts, yet many were the dying messages committed to them and transmitted to loved ones at home. No doubt there are hundreds of gray haired men in all parts of our Southland who remember with gratitude and thanks my mother's administrations at their sick bedside. She made the hospital brighter and more cheery by her presence, and when the angel of death came there came also hope and peace, for she ministered to their spiritual as well as their physical salvation. Can the value of her work be computed or known? Her reward shall be the grateful remembrance of her fellow countrymen and the assurance of her Saviour as He will say to her, "Inasmuch as you did it unto one of the least of these my brethren, you did it unto me." These lines are dedicated to her memory by one of her sons who loves to honor her patriotism, and self-sacrificing conception of duty.

NARROW ESCAPE FROM FEDERAL PRISON
By Mrs. Sue L. James, of Hot Springs

The great Civil War opened its first tragedy on Saturday, April 13, 1861. A few minutes past 12 that morning an old Virginian, Edmund Ruffin, was granted the privilege of firing the first gun on Fort Sumter. Three thousand shells fell in and about the fort and the Union garrison surrendered Sunday, April 14. In the call for troops that was speedily issued my only brother, Ben H. Wills, enlisted in Fagan's First Arkansas Infantry regiment. He served as a flag-bearer until captured when he was sent to Rock Island prison, Ill., where he remained a prisoner until the close of the war. He now sleeps the sleep of the blest.

In the latter part of 1862 Lieut. Henry James, who was my husband, enlisted for service with Capt. Brown's cavalry volunteers, commanded by Gen. Cabell; later he was made adjutant, and put on Col. Monroe's staff. Still later, when Capt. Brown was wounded, he was placed in command of this company, was wounded and captured on the Missouri raid, and sent a prisoner to Johnson's Island with several others of Monroe's regiment, where he remained a prisoner until peace was declared in 1865.

A few months prior to his capture, while Cabell's brigade was stationed near Columbus, Hempstead County, Arkansas, a thrilling incident occurred in my own life which I will relate in as little space as possible.

My husband Lieut. James, had received permission to come with a scout within several miles of Benton, Saline County, Arkansas. He ventured there alone and came to see me and our two baby boys, one eight months, the other two years old.

I was at that time with my mother, Mrs. J. A. McAdoo, formerly Mrs. James M. Wills, where I had refugeed from Little Rock, my home, when the war broke out. It took only a few words of advice from my husband to persuade my mother, then a widow, her husband having died in the army in Mississippi, at Corinth, to send all of her negroes who would go willingly with wagons and horses with myself and children to Texas.

We started within a few hours with the most valuable of our possessions. The scout of fifteen men met Lieut. James just off the old military road from Little Rock to Rockport—on a circuitous one—leading to the Magnet Cove, about seven miles, from old Rockport. We were so heavily loaded it took us a day and a half to get there. We camped out one night and often during the night thought we heard the sound of whispering voices and horses' feet, and as often Lieut. James went with his men to reconnoiter but found it was only the whispering wind or the cautious step of some wild animal. It was about sundown when we reached the Magnet Cove, a lonesome, isolated place, where already the hooting of the owl and scream of the wild beast could be heard, echoing through the dense forest that surrounded it. Only one house could be seen, that of S. Cloud, who married a half sister of my father. To this house we drove up and after greetings with my aunt heard from her the astounding news that the Federal soldiers were all around us, hunting forage and horses and Confederates, too. It took Lieut. James only a few minutes to bid us good-bye and gallop down the lane to where his men had pitched tents for the night.

As I watched his form die away in the gathering gloom I felt that life was indeed a hard problem, and that fate had decreed a dark future for me, yet but a child of sixteen years who had always been shielded from all of life's responsibilities and wants. As I stood there thinking of my husband, brother and relatives, for all I had were in the Confederate service, great tears fell from my eyes to the ground. While I thus stood a party of about 35 Federals, the first I had ever seen, came dashing down the road in the direction of Rockport, and rode up to the gate where I yet stood. With white face and nervous voice I answered their first question (telling a falsehood point blank). I said there had been no rebels around there. Fortunately, when they put the question to Julia, one of the negro women, she answered as I did, but when one of them asked one of the little negro boys, he said "Yes, sir; we seen some back dar," pointing to the way we came. His mother gave him a significant look and said he didn't know what rebel meant and that she had told him as "dey cum along dat way, dat if he don't behave an' quit a-teasin' a coon so (a negro baby), de woods is full of debbils dat looks like men an' dey take him away wid 'em."

This novel explanation, to my surprise and joy, seemed to satisfy them, though the leader looked a little incredulous. He asked all about our journey from Benton, for our wagons stood in front of the gate and the negroes, all but Sam, my mother's trusty, who had saddled one of her fine horses and gone with Lieut. James as his body servant, were huddled about me.

It took only a few hours for the bluecoats to get all the forage in that vicinity, and the next day at 11 o'-clock found us headed for Benton, where only a short time before we had said good-bye and started for Texas. The Federals were very respectful to me all the way, and at no time did they speak to me. Only now and then one more humorous than the rest would laugh at the odd conversation carried on by two negro boys in negro dialect—simon pure.

FEDERALS ENCAMPED AT OLD HOME

Words cannot describe my sensations when at last we drove to my mother's home and saw artillery planted as near the gallery as could be, and all the fences down—with tents stretched all about the yard and or-chard. The large tent was occupied by Col. Ritter of Gen. Steele's division, which now occupied Little Rock. This transformation seemed magical to me, for I had not heard that Gen. Steele's army was in Little Rock nor that Col. Ritter's regiment had come to Benton to stay for an indefinite period. With burning cheek and flashing eye I glanced at the tent next to the side porch, when just then a handsome blond officer, whose epaulettes denoted the rank of colonel came out and, seeing my indignant look and mien, which I supposed amused him, bowed with the grace of an Apollo. This I haughtily resented with a curl of the lip, and a defiant shrug of the shoulders, which he seemed more amused at. I at once strode into my mother's parlor, accompa-nied by my sister, Fannie Wills who, with hidden wrath, showed me all the pictures on the walls, which had been cut in holes and otherwise defaced.

She recounted to me the depredations the soldiers had committed, such as killing the milch cows and calves and chickens and devastating the garden, orchard and stripping the smokehouse. My dear, noble mother did not utter a complaint, though her heart bled for her country and her loved ones and her home. She urged me and sister to be patient and not to do anything that would bring more suffering upon us all.

A BIT OF BRUTALITY

But all the fires of a proud, patriotic Southerner burned and thrilled in our veins, and I fairly gritted my teeth, but held my temper under control when in the presence of the Federals, until one day when I had been exasperated almost beyond endurance, I heard a scream from my baby boy, and then the voice of his nurse Chaney crying "Miss Sue, come here quick." I followed the direction of the voices to the back yard, and there found my baby being held roughly to the ground by a big, rough soldier while another held Julia's negro baby of the same age in his lap, and every now and then made them kiss, at which those around laughed coarsely, and used profane epithets to me and my baby. It seemed to me I jumped from the steps ten feet to where they were. Snatching my baby in my arms, I called on heaven to send judgment and retribution to the cruel cowards. My terrible anger seemed to intimidate them for a time, but later only provoked them to more than profanity, even to blackguardism.

MORE BRUTALITY

After this episode my mother was in constant dread lest I should cause some terrible trouble to come to us all, and she had not long to wait. About a month after the above occurrence we were all aroused one night about 1 o'clock by a succession of guns, fired through our windows, facing the south. My mother, sister Fannie and myself came near being hit several times. As quick as we could we pulled the children all out of bed and with them crawled under the beds for all of us slept in one room, as we were afraid to sleep in different ones. My mother's five children, my half brothers and sisters were all small, and needed almost constant care. At this juncture a loud scream from Julia, the cook, fell on our ears, as the kitchen door burst open and she fell fainting across it. We had no matches nor lamps, and only by the rays of the cold autumn moon could we discover the blood streaming from her mouth and her almost lifeless form, she being enciente, we felt sure she was dead from some awful wound received when the shots were fired. We dragged her in and after a hard rubbing she finally came to and told us how six big burly soldiers had assaulted her. She also said they had Hester, my mother's householdgirl at that time, beating her on the head. Just then Hester came almost lifeless to our room, where Julia had been taken. One eye was closed and four front teeth knocked out, while blood covered her face so that she was almost unrecognizable. At this sight, my mother and myself ran in hot haste to Capt. McCrary's provost marshal's office, where we related in an almost incoherent way what had happened. He snatched his hat and ran ahead of us to our home. I had forgotten to mention that Col. Ritter had been removed to Little Rock, with all his regiment except Capt. McCrary's company of Iowans, and in justice to the captain and the majority of his men I would state that these rough drunken soldiers who had so outraged us and our servants were raw recruits from the low-down foreigners, with one or two half-breeds.

When we arrived home everything was quiet and Capt. McCrary was issuing orders to a corporal to place a guard around our house, which he did, and it was kept there every night for a couple of weeks, as I remember, after which time my mother put a bed in her parlor and Capt. McCrary occupied it until he left. He was a perfect gentleman and deplored the outrages of some of the Federals.

Things went on quite smoothly until one morning while I was sweeping the gallery, a coarse, impudent soldier passed in front of our gate and exposed himself indecently. Now I had with me a little silver mounted pistol my husband had given me when he left for the war, which I had only saved of all my belongings, for a few weeks before some scoundrel had entered our room at night and stolen from under my head a valuable set of garnet and pearl jewelry with my watch and chain and all the gold and silver that I possessed. Well, no sooner than the fellow exposed himself than I snatched from my pocket my pistol and fired two shots at him. He ran for his life and I afterward heard through Mike Curless, a noble young man, whom we all liked, and called "copperhead," a soubriquet often given by us to the more kindly and courteous Federal solders, that the fellow reported me as firing on him while he was peaceably walking past the house. I never did learn what be-

came of him, for Capt. McCrary was ordered to vacate
Benton and rejoin Gen. Steele's army at Little Rock.
The very next day after he left a squad of Confederates
rode into town, but before that the news came that the
Confederates were marching 50,000 strong on to Benton from Camden or near that vicinity, and of all the
running, mounting horses, loading wagons, I have ever
seen, that was the climax. Of course, we were all tickled
almost to death, but had to look on mum, as the report
proved false. However, only a few days elapsed before
the entire company left. I suspect they felt it was a prudent thing to do. As I said, a scout of Confederates
headed by Capt. Gus Crawford, came galloping up to
our house the next day after the Federals left.

"Feds," as they were mostly called, in retaliation for
Rebel. After leisurely riding around to speak to and
look at their relatives, for each man had some there,
some of the men who took care of the horses in the out-
skirts, hidden by bushes and trees, came galloping up to
our back door and my mother and sister Fannie and
myself hurriedly gave them their breakfast, for they had
not eaten since the night before, while recounting to
them the dangers of the Federals at Benton. Mrs. Jane
Elrod, a noble, patriotic woman, who should have a
monument to her memory, came galloping up with the
news that a Federal scout of about one hundred and
fifty men was just outside of Benton. It took only a few
seconds for our men to dash out of sight in the woods
near by. The leading officer of the Federal scout came
galloping up to our house, followed by about fifty men,
and demanded a search of the premises. My mother
consented reluctantly, for underneath the floor in her
room were several blankets and a pair of cavalry boots

which I had bought from the post sutler before Capt. McCrary left Benton and paid fourteen dollars for — paid it in washings, my first time, too. Oh, how I hated to do it, but the boots were of nice patent leather to the knees and I thought they would do my husband so much good. I didn't mind the rubbing of the skin off my hands, that were so tender and white then, but the degradation of washing for men who had robbed us, and who were hunting our loved ones to kill them before our eyes.

But back to my story. I felt a thrill of anger and fear as I saw the soldiers take tools and begin to tear up the floor. I feared only for my mother, as I did not care what became of me at that moment. They tore up the floor in the parlor, walked straight to mother's room and began to tear up the floor. Great heavens! they would soon reveal the blankets and boots, the contraband goods hidden there, and then what? I stood pale and scornful watching them, within my heart saying, "Go ahead and do your best; I am not afraid of you." One plank ripped up, another, another. I looked at mother and sister, pale but speechless. At last I cried out: "They are there with guns to shoot you." They took no notice of this further than to go a little slower, and now that there was room for a man to crawl through several knelt down and peered under the house, and seeing no one, but seeing a heap of dirt in the little dark cellar, they crawled quickly in and began digging, expecting to find a live rebel or a dead Federal, I know not which. The mound was a covering for our contraband goods. "Oh, my boots will go, mother," I whispered. She, pale and quiet, gave me a reproving look. This the soldiers did not hear or see.

"Now they have them all," I said hopelessly. But lo! when the dirt was removed there was nothing but dirt; where were the blankets and boots? The good Father must have sent an angel to spirit them away and save us from prison, I said to mother. She looked at me as much astonished as I was. Well, the search was over at last and the last rays of the setting sun had flung showers of shimmering gold athwart the quiet little town of Benton as if to shed a final brightness over our sad hearts and homes.

That night we all went to bed hungry. The Federals' frequent trips had stripped us of everything to eat almost and when they left we had only a pittance of bread and of meat.

GOOD MIKE CURLESS

But one week from that night will long be remembered by us all, for at the hour of 10 that night Mike Curless, who had been permitted to come with the scout, rode in haste to our house and told us that we had been reported for harboring and feeding rebels and sending contrabrand goods to their army; also that I was to be taken to Alton, Ill., as a prisoner for attempting to kill a United States soldier. He didn't know at what time, but he knew I was to go soon and after urging secrecy galloped down to the court house, where some of the scout had dismounted. My mother was almost frantic now and we sat up or walked the floor until daybreak when our joy was to behold five of our men ride up to door and ask if there were any "Feds" about. We told them a scout had been there early in the evening, but had gone back to Little Rock. Then my mother poured out our fears to them, when to our surprise they said they had come to notify me that one of Cabell's men was waiting about a mile distant to carry me to Cabell's headquarters near Columbus, Hempstead County. Jack Lecroy was the man who had been detailed by Gen. Cabell at the request of Lieut. James to bring an ambulance for me and my babies and take us to their headquarters.

We were so astonished we could not speak at once. Then I cried out: "Who told them I was to be sent a prisoner to Alton, Ill?

Had Rowen, one of Capt. Crawford's men, said: "It seems a fellow by the name of Mike Curless informed Mrs. Jane Elrod and she sent a letter to Lieut. James notifying him. Mrs. Elrod told me to tell you that the boots were received by Lieut. James, and also one blanket by Col. Monroe."

She had met a scout out on the old military road nine miles south of Benton and delivered them the boots and the blanket. She also told him how she had crawled under the house, when she saw the Federals coming, and pulled the blankets and boots out, and tied the boots under her hoop skirts, which were roomy, and put one blanket under her saddle with her old one used for a blanket, so that it could not be detected. The other blankets—there were three—she partly spread between the quilts on a bed in a room next to the kitchen while the Federals were ripping up the planks, and then she sat down on the gallery, seemingly a visitor for the day. My sister Fannie and I clapped our hands in delight, while my mother said seriously: "Surely the workings of Providence are strange, but altogether right."

But now our boys were gone to tell Mr. Lecroy I would be ready by 8 o'clock that night, and he must come to the edge of the woods, about one hundred and fifty yards from our orchard, and get some one to help him carry my trunk to the ambulance. All day my mother watched the street leading toward Little Rock, ever and anon saying "Hush! I hear horses' hoofs," but 8 o'clock came and no "Feds" had been there. Silently but tearfully we bade each other good-bye and I was soon riding behind a pair of strong mules toward Hempstead County, where my husband awaited my coming with the little boys, tremulously and anxiously. We had gone but nine miles when the left wheel broke down and Mr. Lecroy was forced to improvise one by cutting a strong sapling, fastening one end to the front axle and letting the other drag. This compelled me to sit with my youngest child on my lap and the other holding tightly to my dress while I leaned forward and held hard to the standard or post on the right of the ambulance, a most cramped and miserable position. Mr. Lecroy tried to cheer us all the way, but he had no time to delay, as Federal scouts might at any time overtake us, and either kill him or imprison us all.

The roads were awfully bad and our first night out we had to sit up in a log cabin. The owner was a poor woman with five dirty children, her husband in the war, and she had only fat meat and cornmeal. I tried to cook my first meal, but made such a miserable failure that Mr. Lecroy came to my rescue and finished after I had blistered my hands and almost burnt my face.

After a narrow escape from drowning in a swollen slough we at last arrived on the third day at the camp, where I at once became the heroine of a number of old

Tige's men, as he was familiarly called. He, Gen. Cabell, complimented me on my bravery, and Mr. Lecroy on his strategy. Here at last I found happiness once more, and often rode horseback with my old soldier friends or watched the brigade on dress parade.

My happiness did not last long, however. In a few weeks Gen. Cabell with his brigade was ordered away, and I was forced to go farther south. I went to Mr. James' cousin's plantation at Dercheat, Union County, the home of Maj. D. O. Kyle, where I remained until Mr. Bromley came for me and accompanied me back to the "Clift place" five miles from Benton, where my mother and sister Fannie Wills, with the rest of the children, had refugeed after our home in Benton was burned.

A NICETY OF BRUTALITY

That was the time my mother had been taken prisoner at daybreak, one cold, sleety morning and marched in her gown, barefooted, to a Federal wagon, where she was placed before the house was fired and driven a mile on their way to Little Rock, when the Federal soldiers told her to look back at her home. She looked back and saw forked flames that seemed to lick the sky, when one of the men began to curse her and said: "Your d—d rebel young ones are burned up." She did not know any better until after she reached Little Rock. Chief Justice English, his wife and Miss Sophia Crease met my mother in a carriage with a permit obtained ingeniously from Gen. Steele to allow her to remain a prisoner at the home of Chief Justice English, where she was guarded until, by the repeated efforts of those chivalric and patriotic friends, she was released and after repeated efforts had been made to administer to her the oath of allegiance. My sisters and brothers were all kindly cared for by friends in Benton, after the home was burned, until her release.

It would take pages to tell all of our experiences during that sad war. Memory takes me back to those days, moves me, possesses me until I again live in the days that are dead. I hear again the murmur of Saline river and the low roll of drums from the surrounding forest, where camps of infantry and cavalry are aroused by the "reveille." In the breeze I seem to hear the bugles, and thundering roar of artillery as we breathlessly wait for news of our loved ones. At Shiloh I see again our loved ones who used to wear the gray and march under the red flag of the South to die on a couch of blood, and whose only requiem was the swell and moan of the autumnal winds, whose shroud only the variegated autumn leaves. I hear again like the burst of thunder "Old Tige is advancing"—a quick throb of the heart and exclamation of joy as we clasp our arms about a phantom form. Alas! to find that it was only a dream.

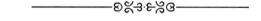

WORK OF MRS. JAMES M. KELLER,
OF HOT SPRINGS
By J. M. Lucey

The life of Mrs. Keller became entwined in the war record of the Confederate soldiers of Arkansas in various ways, due largely to the fact that her husband, Dr. James M. Keller, was medical director of the Trans-

Mississippi Department of the Confederacy. In the first years of the war she frequently accompanied him on the expeditions, which his official duties required him to make. In this way, Mrs. Keller became known to the Arkansas divisions of the army and her womanly influence cast a charm over many dismal scenes of camp life.

In the Confederate hospitals of Memphis, which she was chiefly instrumental in founding, many Arkansas soldiers were nursed back to life and restored to the ranks of the Southern army. From the close of the war in 1865, to the time of her death at Hot Springs, April 8, 1906, she was a most enthusiastic and successful worker and organizer of Chapters of the Daughters of the Confederacy.

Mrs. Keller, a native of Kentucky, and a member of one of the most prominent families of the bluegrass region, was born, August 31, 1831, in Jefferson County, not far from Louisville. She was a graduate of Nazareth Academy, Nelson County. Her maiden name was Sallie Phillips. When about twenty years of age, she married Dr. James M. Keller, and in 1901, the golden jubilee of their wedding was happily celebrated at Hot Springs, Ark.

In the progress of the Civil war, Mrs. Keller, finding that her stay in Memphis might continue for a considerable length of time through force of circumstances, set to work to improve the Overton Hotel hospital, and then organized the old State hospital, where the Dominican Sisters of the Catholic church were placed in charge. It is not possible in a brief sketch to describe the wonderful work of this noble woman in these and other hospitals during the gloomy days and nights when the pall of Southern defeat was gathering over them like a bird of evil prey. The courage of Southern womanhood was never more severely tested, and their heroic conduct never more beautifully illustrated than when they went forth at early morn from their own lonely homes to remain until late at night beside the cot of the dying Southern soldier. And among the women who distinguished themselves in the terrible ordeal, Mrs. Keller was preeminent. Her intuitive knowledge of elementary medical practice, her maternal heart and ardent Southern nature made her presence something to be watched for and greeted with the grateful expression of eye when tongue was silent.

In the Confederate hospitals of Memphis, there were numerous cases of extraordinary interest: A youth of tender years whose delirium was about a loving mother; a soldier who was brought in merely to die in comfort and who surprised doctors and nurses by living; officers, whose impatience to return to their commands and win promotion by bravery on the battlefield, taxed the patience of every attendant. All these incidents were looked upon as matters of course and no records were kept, but the brave men of the commands of General Patrick Cleburne and of General Nathan Bedford Forest, carried away the images of the ministering angels of the hospitals as their happiest mementoes.

The standing of Mrs. Keller in the army of the enemy may be estimated from the fact that the very first thing which the Federal commander did after the capture of Memphis was to exile her and her two small children to the malarial swamp below the city. It was supposed that she could not survive with life, so close was the environment. This forecast would no doubt have proven true but for the vigilance and fidelity of a negro slave whose ingenuity rescued her from this frightful captivity and enabled her to rejoin her husband.

With the close of the war, the family moved to Hot Springs, Ark., when her active nature and strong Southern feeling led her to the front in all the work of women for the consecration in memoriam of the deeds of the heroes and heroines of the lost cause. Mrs. Keller was instrumental in founding the organization of the Chapters of the Daughters of the Confederacy throughout the South and at the time of her death she was the honorary president of the national association. She was frequently president of the Arkansas State Chapter and the J. M. Keller Chapter of Little Rock was so named in her honor. Her husband standing even now like the stalwart oak of the forest after the storm cloud has passed, firmer and stronger in the possession of earthly life and yet lonely enough except for the images of the past, reveres her memory as the benediction of his life. He loves her most who knew her best.

————————☙❧————————

BRAVERY OF MRS CLAY ROBINSON
By Mrs. J. C. Poindexter, of Imboden

As my mother Mrs. Clay Robinson, is not living to help write the history of "Woman in the War," I will give you a few instances of which I have heard her often talk.

She carried a message from Clover Bend to Jacksonport or near there to Gen. Dandrige McRae, who was at that time with his command at Jacksonport. I think this message was from Gen. Sterling Price. The courier who started with it to Jacksonport was taken suddenly very sick and was compelled to stop at Kinion's at Clover Bend. My mother was there visiting. When she learned the state of affairs and that it was very necessary that the dispatch reach Gen. McRae within a few hours, she offered to take the dispatch to Gen. McRae for him. The courier told her that it was too great an undertaking, as she would be risking her life, to say nothing of the loss of the dispatches, should she be captured. She told him she was willing to run the risk and would give her life before surrendering the dispatch, if he would trust her.

She was then 21 years old and was the widow of Clay Robinson, who had died a short time before from measles and exposure contracted in the army.

Finally the soldier gave her the dispatch and told her to take it to Bob Gray near Jacksonport, a distance of about 30 miles.

She was accompanied by a young lady, I believe it was Miss Emma Kinion, who is now Mrs. Ben Bush and lives two miles below Clover Bend. They started late in the evening and when about 10 miles from home they met two men. The women rode on the shady side of the road. The moon was shining and one said "Good evening, gentlemen." The other whistled a hymn as they passed. When they were a few yards past, the men stopped and one of them said "halt!" but the women rode on as if they had not heard the command. The men then started on and there was nothing more to distress them except the dread of being captured, and with them the dispatch. Weary and worn out from riding so far,

they reached Gray's home some time before daylight.
The dispatch was turned over to Mr. Gray and reached
Gen. McRae safely.

HELD AS SPY

In 1864 my mother was taken prisoner, suspected of
being a Confederate spy. She was at her uncle's (Col. J
A. Lindsay), and was getting on her horse to go home
(Clover Bend), a distance of six miles, when two men
rode up, one on each side, and told her to consider herself under arrest. She asked why she was arrested and
was told that she was too far from home and it was suspected that she was in search of information for the
Southern army. She told them that she was looking for
her brother's horse, that the Yankees had stolen and
had heard that it had been seen near Lindsay's and she
had come to see about it, but of course this had no
weight with them. By this time she had been forced to
ride into line as the regiment was passing. They were
going in the direction of her home, therefore, she didn't
mind so much going with them as she would had they
been going the opposite direction. When the colonel of
the regiment came up to where she was, she asked him
what he intended to do with her, and he said: "Take you
to Jacksonport and try you." She said: "There is, no
one at Jacksonport that knows me at all; at home is the
place to try me where I am known." She told him she
wouldn't go to Jacksonport. He might bind her hand
and foot and take her, but she positively would not go
any other way. He then asked her if she would take the
oath not to assist the Confederacy. She said: "If that is
the only way of release I will;" then said he "Will you be

true to the oath?" She replied: "No, sir, I would not consider it worth the snap of my finger after you are out of sight." The colonel became convinced that he could not get evidence against her, so when they reached her home (a very short distance) he released her.

RICH HAUL BY THIEVES

One day some men came to Mamma's home and claimed to be in search of arms. They went through everything except a trunk which they could not open. Mamma told them there was nothing of the kind in the trunk and refused to open it, but when one of them got an ax and threatened to burst it open (it was a steel frame and covered with leather) she opened it rather than have it ruined. She took the contents out, one article at a time until she came to a sack of money (gold and silver) which she knew was what they were after. She had not more than got hold of it until one man grabbed it out of her hands. It became untied and the coin was scattered over the floor. The man raked it up in his hands. Mamma said to him, "I wouldn't ask you for a cent of it to save your life except that five dollar gold piece with the blue ribbon on it. It belongs to this child, (putting her hand on her four-year-old boy, who was standing near by, and hadn't said a word, although there were tears in his eyes). His grandfather gave it to him the day he was a year old." The man said, "Oh, well that will buy me a breakfast some morning," and left the house.

When she moved the trunk she found that a quarter had slipped under the trunk, which was the only cent on the place.

The same day three other men came to the house. One of them asked mamma what was fastened to that cord she was wearing around her neck. She told him it was none of his business. He took hold of the cord and mamma picked up a hammer which was lying on the stair case close by and struck him on the head. As he dodged from the lick the cord was broken, also the skin on her neck in more than one place. The watch fell on the hearth; mamma got hold of it first. She wrapped the cord around her wrist and held the watch out toward him and said: "When you get this watch you will take it off my dead body." She was a small woman, her average weight being about 115 pounds, but was bravery itself. She would have fought for the watch, because it was formerly her husband's. It is an old gold hunting case and a good watch yet. (My husband is carrying it.) The man turned and walked out. One of the other men said: "She bluffed you, did she?" Ma said: "and you two are no part of gentlemen or you wouldn't stand by and see a woman imposed on." They said, "Oh, we didn't want to have anything to do with it."

My mother was originally Mary Scanlan and lived with Col. J. A. Lindsay from childhood (as her parents died when she was small), until 1858, when she married Clay Robinson. In 1869 she married Dr. B. F. Austin, who was Captain of Co. G. in Freeman's old regiment. She died April 8, 1902.

JOHN WISE AND HIS BIG CLOTHES

The spectacle presented at the social gatherings, particularly the starvation parties, was picturesque in the extreme. The ladies often took down the damask and other curtains and made dresses of them. My friend, Hon. John S. Wise, formerly of Virginia, now of New York, tells the following story of himself: He was serving in front of Richmond and was invited to come into the city to attend a starvation party. Having no coat of his own fit to wear, he borrowed one from a brother officer nearly twice his height. The sleeves of his coat covered his hands entirely, the skirt came below his knees several inches, and the buttons in the back were down on his legs. So attired, Captain Wise went to the party. His first partner in the dance was a young lady of Richmond belonging to one of its best families. She was attired in the dress of her great-grandmother, and a part of this dress was a stomacher very suggestive in its proportions. Captain Wise relates with exquisite humor that the sight presented by himself and his partner was so ridiculous that he burst out laughing; and his partner turned and looked at him angrily, left his side and never spoke to him, again.

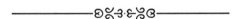

ORIGIN OF CONFEDERATE MEMORIAL ASSOCIATION

The New York Herald contains the following contribution from Mrs. John A. Logan, in which she says that the "Decoration Day" in the North was an adoption from the South's "Memorial Day."

To the Editor of the Herald:

In the spring of 1868, General Logan and I were invited to visit the battle-grounds of the South with a party of friends. As certain important matters kept him from joining the party, however, I went alone, and the trip proved a most interesting and impressive one. The South had been desolated by the war. Everywhere signs of privation and devastation were constantly presenting themselves to us. The graves of the soldiers however, seemed as far as possible the objects of the greatest care and attention.

One graveyard that struck me as being especially pathetic was in Richmond. The graves were new, and just before our visit there had been a "Memorial Day" observance, and upon each grave had been placed a small Confederate flag and wreaths of beautiful flowers. The scene seemed most impressive to me, and when I returned to Washington I spoke of it to the General and said I wished there could be concerted action of this kind all over the North for the decoration of the graves of our own soldiers. The General thought it a capital idea, and with enthusiasm set out to secure its adoption.

At that time be was commander-in-chief of the Grand Army. The next day he sent for Adjutant-General Chipman, and they conferred as to the best means of beginning a general observance. On the 5th day of May in that year the historic order was put out. General Logan often spoke of the issuing of this order as the proudest act of his life.

It was marvelous how popular the idea became. The papers all over the land copied the order, and the observance was a general one. The memorial ceremonies that took place at Arlington that year were perfectly inspiring to all the old soldiers. Generals Grant, Sherman, and Sheridan and many of those who have since passed away attended the first solemn observance of that day.

MRS. JOHN A. LOGAN

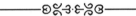

PERSONAL RECOLLECTIONS
By Mrs. Josephine Robinson Brandenburg, of Jacksonport

Mrs. Josephine Robinson Brandenburg, who is a native of Jackson County, Arkansas, thinks because she did not live in the midst of battle-fields and was not near the seat of war that her experiences are of little worth. But as it is easier for soldiers to go to the front than it is to stay in the back ground and wait, so it was much harder for those poor anxious women to wait and watch and work without any news for many long months often, from their loved ones, who were fighting afar off, than it was for those who were nearer the conflict and could not have time to think. In speaking of the days spent in these long lonely years, Mrs. Brandenburg says: "We were fortunate in not being in the thickest of the fight I presume, but we, notwithstanding this, went through a great many hardships and untold anxieties. At the beginning of the war my home was in Jacksonport from which place the Jacksonport Guards went out. I assisted in making their flag, which they so proudly carried away, so faithfully protected, and though "tattered and torn," they brought it back after having followed it for four years. During the second year of the war, my father, James Robinson, with my mother, myself, and several true and tried slaves, moved to our plantation, about ten miles from Jacksonport, where we spent the remainder of the time till the war closed. My father was then 63 years old. Our house was many times a haven of refuge for our soldiers. Once when the Federal soldiers were known to be in our vicinity, a girl, Miss Pink Weatherly, daughter of Capt. Weatherly, and I stood for hours, at either end of the lane in front of our house "watching for the Yankees," while my mother cooked a midnight supper for some of our own boys. We spent most of our days spinning, weaving and making garments and smuggling them to our soldiers at every opportunity, but sending them at great risk. At one time this same Jacksonport girl came to our house and on finding that we had several woolen suits of underwear, socks, etc., ready to send away, she insisted that we put them all on her that she might wear them and go through the Federal lines and take them to our soldiers. I believe that she succeeded in getting on nine suits of these clothes and when she reached Jacksonport, she was given some valuable papers to be taken with her. She reached her destination safely but was months in returning home again. After the battle of Pea Ridge, Lieut. Green Brandenburg (afterwards my husband) sent to me a letter telling of his safety, and that his company had been dismounted and that he had sent to me his pony. This horse was brought by a colored boy, "Dick," who belonged to me, but who gladly went into the Confederate army and staid until the war ended. This pony was the cause of much anxiety on my part, for I constantly feared that the "Yankees" would get him. I remember to have sat on him a whole day once to keep them from taking him off. They got to be very insulting and I thought once I would have to give him up, but they finally went away promising to return that night. After a long night's watching, I decided that they had been joking, and were not coming for the horse, for that time at least. The pony lived to do us good service long after the war closed. I helped my poor old father to count and securely pack twelve thousand dollars in gold to be sent to Little Rock, by James K. Polk Pritchard, to be turned over to the Confederacy. I remember to have seen the receipt for this money in very recent years. It was all we had left, but we gave it so proudly and gladly.

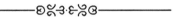

SKETCH OF MRS. D. H. REYNOLDS, OF LAKE VILLAGE
By Mrs. J. W. McMurray

Mrs. D. H. Reynolds, the subject of this sketch, was a Miss Wallace, born in Holmes County, Mississippi in 1845; moved to Arkansas in 1859, and shared in the fortunes of our State during the war and reconstruction period. She met General Reynolds in Lake Village soon after his return from the war, in which he had lost a leg, shot off by a cannon ball at Bentonville, N. C., in the last important battle of the war. They were married in 1868, a lovely uniting of two fine characters. The General accepted the results of the war in the spirit of our heroes, resumed his law practice at Lake Village and invested in land of Chicot County to the amount, at one time, of about sixty thousand acres, in the mapping and platting of which Mrs. Reynolds developed a correct and artistic talent. Their home on Lake Chicot was presided over by Mrs. Reynolds with sweet grace and was the center of generous hospitality. General Albert Pike and Attorney General A. H. Garland and other prominent members of the Arkansas bar, were always at home there and as long as they lived cherished the recollection of the hospitality they had enjoyed.

Mrs. Reynolds is the mother of five children, the eldest, Mrs. Joseph Hill, wife of our Chief Justice, Robert W., who sacrificed his young life and promising manhood in his country's cause, being first Lieutenant in the Thirteenth Cavalry U. S. A., and dying in the U. S. hospital at Hot Springs in 1906, shortly after his return from two years service in the Philippines. The second daughter, Eleanor, is unmarried and a third, Ruth is now the wife of Mr. Frank Bull, assistant cashier in the Chicot bank; these with Daniel H. Jr., the youngest son, all survive to bless the declining years of their devoted mother.

These are only a few dry facts in the life of our friend, but they form the framework of a picture that lives in the hearts of those who know her best. A picture from which shines out a generosity only limited by her means and a charity that "suffereth long and is kind," that "thinketh no evil," "rejoices not in iniquity but rejoices in the truth."

The chairman of the Arkansas memorial committee may add to this beautiful sketch of Mrs. Reynolds, the fact that the flag of General Reynold's brigade is now in the Richmond museum, having been purchased from Colorbearer Daglan Foley by him and presented to the Arkansas room of the museum.

--------------⊗⅗·3·⅗⅔⊛--------------

SAM C. BELL AND CHARLES SCOTT
By Mrs. Mary E. Woodruff Bell, of Little Rock

In the year 1863, Charles Scott, who had moved with his family from Van Buren to Little Rock, was in Baltimore with his daughters, Misses Emma and Johanna Scott. One morning he left the hotel before breakfast, to go to the market, telling the young ladies that he would return in time for breakfast. He was away so long, that his daughters became uneasy lest some accident had befallen him; the father returned, however, safe enough, but whispered the exciting news that he had seen a Confederate soldier, Col. Sam S. Bell, whom he had known in Little Rock. The soldier had gone into a restaurant for a cup of coffee or such a breakfast as his slim purse would allow. The two men recognized one another at once, but, with a glance, Col. Bell made Mr. Scott understand that they must not speak. With the ingenuity that comes to all in time of necessity they managed to meet in confidence and Mr. Scott learned that Col. Bell and nine other prisoners of war (including his brother, Capt. Jo. Bell) were being taken from Johnson's Island to Point Lookout. Knowing what that meant, all of them determined to make their escape, which they did. The two brothers jumped from the train just before it reached Baltimore, neither one knowing that the other had escaped. After talking with each other as long as they thought prudent to do so, Mr Scott handed the soldier a roll of bills, knowing that he must be ill-prepared for a long journey. Col. Bell thankfully accepted the money saying that he would "make it good" when he arrived at Little Rock. The friends parted, one to go on to Philadelphia, where he placed his daughters in Mrs. Cagey's school, making five of Little Rock's young girls there, Mrs. Myra (McAlmont) Vaughan, of Little Rock; Mrs. Laura (Tucker) Hardy, of Chicago; Mrs. Lizzie (Reynolds) Fellows, of New York; Mrs. Emma (Scott) Lawson, of Little Rock, and the late Johanna (Scott) Roberts of Little Rock.

The escaped prisoners were taken in and hidden at the home of the proprietor of a gents' furnishing house in Baltimore. Col. Bell often expressed regret that the name of the family escaped his memory, for after the troublesome times were over he longed to write and thank them for their kindness. But he was glad, after the surrender, on his return to Little Rock, to find his generous hearted friend and returned the money which proved so helpful.

Col. Bell afterward married Miss Mary Woodruff, daughter of the late Wm. E. Woodruff, Sr., of Little Rock. His brother was sick at a Catholic hospital in Baltimore and the two met at their home at Hamburg, Ashley County, Ark., their first meeting since leaving Johnson's Island. What became of the other soldiers who escaped, they never knew.

SIGN OF THE STORK

A young captain of our country, himself a married man, read and wrote letters for many of his men unable to read or write. He told me of opening a letter at the request of a sturdy young soldier who had left a young wife at home. There was nothing of special moment in the letter, but the soldier blushed and laughed when the captain held up a blue yarn string and said, "What does this mean, Rodgers, a secret token from your wife?" "Yes, captain, that means good news." Months after, returning from a furlough, the young soldier came to his captain and said, "I left a young soldier boy at home, sir, and we've named him Robt. E. Lee."

"Rodgers," said the captain, "was that the yarn string token?" "Yes, captain, that was it."

———————— ⊗⅋·3·ᙓ·⅍⊕ ————————

REMINISCENCES OF THE OLD SOUTH
By Mrs. Elmira F. Snodgrass, of Little Rock

In the strong light of the twentieth century, it is sometimes difficult to bring from the sleeping past, facts that are imprinted not only upon marble tablets or on history's page, but upon the fleshy human heart as well. To some of us these remembrances are as undying, as what occurred is beyond recall.

The decade reaching from 1850 to 1860 as time is computed holds in its grasp a living picture that extends from the outer boundary of the Southland to its magnificent unmarred center. No language is so full of poetry or so fragrant with the flowers of Rhetoric as to graphically describe the "Old South," as we, the silver-haired devotees, remember it. The country itself was a resplendent setting, planned and completed by creative power for the courtly, cultured, magnanimous men, and the refined, modest, virtuous women who composed her loyal citizenship. Like one of the fixed stars in midnight firmament which glows on forever unsullied, so the old South preeminently adorns the picture gallery of memory. Fleet-winged time marked the receding days; with the early sixties there appeared upon the political horizon of our country a cloud, perhaps no larger than a man's hand, but which eventually proved to be a beacon of destruction to the aggrandizement and accumulation of years, as well as the destroyer of ideal homes, the crushing of women's hearts and the bringing of our dearest ones to coffinless graves. For many hours we could deal in generalities, yet, not exhausting the terrorizing tenths that burn like a blazing censor upon the historic scroll of '61 to '65. Personally, it seemed at first that the war was far off; we heard the bugle call, saw our gallant young men arrayed in handsome grey uniforms, march away at officer's command, but no picture of things that awaited us had been outlined on our mental sky.

In January, 1862, the fertile plains of what is known as the tobacco belt of west Kentucky, first reverberated with the alarming tocsin of war. Our beautiful homes resting on the peaceful landscape like children in the sheltered havens of a well appointed nursery dreamed not of danger or wreckage. At sunset that cold winter day the hurried message came. Smith and Wallace's army, 5,000 strong, are marching through from Mayfield to Fort Donaldson on Tennessee river. They are sweeping everything in their course. We had scarcely heard the news, when the shrill bugle call and the drum's thunderous alarm confirmed the truth. With fire and sword they came. Leisurely they passed on taking everything that could be consumed or destroyed. In four days and nights, (the terror of which will never be forgotten) they had swept like a cyclone our beautiful country. My own loved home, magnificent in proportions and restful as a dream of Eden was literally devastated. Our negro houses with their entire contents were burned to the ground turning the poor creatures out in the deluge of rain and sleet with nothing but their usual wearing apparel. The dwelling was wrecked, my aged parents and myself were left shelterless and bedless. Not a living animal or fowl, or morsel of food of the bountiful year's provisions laid in was left, when Smith and Wallace's army had gone. A girl of eighteen summers untouched by any rough wind or torrid sun, the petted child of luxury, filled with high and holy ambitions, in this brief space found herself without resource, yet, the caretaker of her aged and afflicted parents and the supervisor of a multitude of dependent negroes who had never known a want of comfort nor ever felt a responsibility. God only knows how we lived through it! Gen. Lew Wallace would have to write many "Ben Hurs," many tales founded upon the Christ, before my deadened sense of his goodness would be resuscitated. My experience is only a prototype of many others in dear old Kentucky, which was unfortunately the foraging ground for both armies. In July, 1863, a skirmish between Confederate and Federal cavalry occurred at Lashers, a church near my home. Col. Hawkins commanding five hundred Federal cavalry, stopping at the noon hour, had placed his pickets and they were resting nicely, when Capt. Ward, who with a small squad of men dashed from a thick covert of woods through their lines and fired into the main body, causing a perfect stampede; Ward's men turned and followed their Captain at breakneck speed through the lane into the thick woods beyond. Hawkins' men came after them yelling and firing their guns in wildest confusion. The bullets fell like hail on the roof and porches singing about our ears as myself and the negroes thoughtless of danger ran out to see the chase. The Federals did not go in pursuit of Capt. Ward for they were sure the whole woods were full of Rebels. When they turned, a captain of the Federals dashed up to the gate. I was still on the front porch; he commanded me to tell him where I had those Rebels hidden. I replied I did not have them hidden. I did not know Captain Ward was in the country at all. He became furious; he cursed me until he could find no words wicked enough to express himself, then he threatened to kill me and burn the house over me; I did not move, I was utterly in his power, so I told him to kill me if he would, but I had told the truth; at this juncture, "Old Dafney," our dear old colored mammy came in view; she ran to him crying, "Mister, Mister, hold on—Miss Mira is telling you de God's truth! We ain't had no soldiers here!" He turned to her saying, "Well, Aunty, if you say so, I will take your word, but I won't believe that Secesh gal." He then rode away, followed by the men who had been waiting for orders. During the whole war my life was one bitter dream of horror. I was imperiled in three or four skirmishes where the bullets fell around me like hail and the shrieks of the wounded and dying froze my blood with horror. I have at the point of a bayonet cooked for the Yankees until there was nothing left that could be cooked. Utterly unprotected I knew not at what hour I might suffer personal violence.

I cannot write these facts coldly, I cannot speak them calmly, the wound has never healed, and when touched the abrasion shows acute inflammation. Dear hearts, I am making you tired, but my life was potent with golden dreams, which that cruel war turned into hydra form. The scenes we forget are not erased. While the engulfing tide of circumstances implunge the past in texture of new design, yet, in the nightime when the winds sigh around the corners, when stray, restless birds sing piteous notes, or a distant bell tinkles, when shadows play fitfully across the window pane, thought untrammeled flies down the dim penumbra of the past, bringing again to life the scenes that were graven on our hearts when life was young. The Federal army robbed my children of their rights before they were born! The Old South with all its resources was theirs by inheritance, but in lieu of its advantages, they have been made a part of the brick and mortar worked into the building of the New South. The precious darlings of a former generation lie coffinless on many a battlefield, the darlings of this generation, full of the Spartan blood of the mothers of the new South, stand invincible in the faith of the ultimate glory of the new principle for which our country surrendered its all. Dead bodies are not all that await a resurrection to immortal life! Principles founded on God's eternal truth, though crushed to earth hold the germ of Divinity, and can never die. Some time a paean of victory will be sounded, coming from all over this great republic, yea the voices from hundreds of battlefields will write in proclaiming the righteous laurels of our South, and the glorifying of Him who said: "Not by power, not by might, but by my spirit cometh victory."

The hopes so fondly cherished lie
Deep buried in the misty past,
Crushed, yet they cannot die
Their merit is so vast.

Let me dream of their beauty,
The joy of their pristine life;
To reillume by my duty
The charm with which they are rife.

I cannot shut out the glory,
That covered life's morning,
Nor darken the gilded story,
That grew in its roseate dawning.

Oh youth! the elusive maiden
Has slipped unbidden away,
But gems with which she was laden
Are my treasures today.

Resplendent in virtue supernal
They long shut in my bosom
Will spring into life eternal
Crowning the theme I have chosen.

We look on the New South today,
With pride in its success take part,
But O, the Old South is hidden away,
In every Old Southerner's heart.

JEFFERSON DAVIS MONUMENT

The project to erect an appropriate monument to the great Chieftain of the Confederacy was undertaken by the veterans years ago. They raised about $20,000. The Daughters of the Confederacy, just as they always do, then took hold of the matter and they increased the fund to $70,000. The Georgia United Daughters of the Confederacy, who built a Winnie Davis dormitory at the Georgia Normal School, have been very active in the work for the Davis monument at Richmond, and Georgia has the credit of leading all the States in the amount contributed. The city of Richmond donated a very eligible lot at the crossing of Franklin and Cedar streets, near the splendid R. E. Lee monument. It is fitting that the monuments to the leading civil and military heroes of the great cause shall be so near each other. Very near to these will be monuments each to Gen. J. E. B. Stuart, and to Gen. Fitz Hugh Lee. These monuments will all stand in the Lee district, the new and coming choice residence section of the glorious city.

This splendid monument to Mr. Davis was unveiled at the Confederate reunion in 1907. Dirt was formally broken on the 7th of November, 1905 by Mrs. Thomas McCullough, of Staunton, president of the Davis Monument Association. Hon. J. Taylor Ellyson, lieutenant governor elect, a noble veteran, and others, also took part in the historic ceremonies. The picks and shovels will be preserved in the Confederate museum.

SKETCH OF MRS. JARED C. MARTIN
By Miss Mollie D. Martin, of Little Rock

Mrs. Mary Martin was born near Gallatin, Tenn., January 10, 1809. Her parents, John and Sarah Douglass, with other relatives came in a keel boat to Arkansas territory in 1819. They settled near where Little Rock has since been built. There was only one little log cabin here then, and it was occupied by the man who ran the ferry boat, and was near a spring that is in the old state house grounds.

In this sparsely settled country Mary Douglass grew up. She improved the few opportunities of attending the country schools; she had a remarkable memory, and could talk for hours of the old settlers, all over the State, and of her large connection in Tennessee. Here in her happy home she was married to Jared C. Martin, January 25, 1827. They built a comfortable home in Pulaski County and raised a large family. Her husband died November 7, 1857, and the care of her children and slaves devolved on her; she bravely did her best to make all dependent on her comfortable and happy. She was a sincere Christian, and sang sweet old sacred songs as she went about her household work. Her beloved father, John Douglass, died January, 1861. She was very desolate with husband and father both gone; but the dark days of war came soon and there was not time to think of self, or our own trouble. Her husband had been a patriotic, public spirited man, and had often said to her that he feared a civil war was coming soon, and he thought a war with some foreign nation would be a blessing in uniting the people of the United States. She loved quiet and peace, and the idea of war was dreadful, but when it came there was no one more willing to do all she could for the Confederate soldiers. Her home was just two miles from Little Rock, near the river. The Confederate army often camped in a wooded part of the farm; they called the place Camp Texas. Her home was a home for Confederate soldiers and often it was crowded with the sick. She nursed them and cared for them tenderly, she said their mothers had worked and cared for them, and it seemed dreadful for them to be neglected when they were sick and wounded. Some of the wounded from the fight of Cotton Plant stopped awhile at her house, and one wounded man stayed three months; he recovered and went to his command. Some were very sick and three from Texas died. In the spring of 1863 her dear old home had to be abandoned. The line of breast works that Gen. Price had built below Little Rock extended entirely across her farm, her houses and every improvement were entirely destroyed, cotton burned, a hundred and thirty bales, and with her younger children she sought refuge in an old place she had ten miles southwest of Little Rock. Here she and her four children toiled as they never had before, plowing, hoeing, harvesting, cooking, washing, spinning, weaving, and often after they had succeeded in raising a little crop, the enemy came and took it all. She had a wagon and a yoke of oxen, the only wagon and team in the neighborhood, and the women living near brought their grain to her house, and she sent it eight miles to mill for them. She was a fine manager and her family never suffered for the necessaries of life, and when Confederate scouts would occasionally come, she always had something for them to eat and if they were in need of clothes she would find some for them. Her two grown sons were in the army and the servants all gone, stock of every description had been taken. She never despaired but worked on trusting in God for help and comfort.

When the cruel war was over with nothing but the land left, in her old age, she had to begin to gather up something to make a home again; she worked bravely for a few years, and was taken to her reward February 14, 1877.

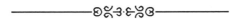

ARKANSAS SISTERS OF MERCY IN THE WAR
By J. M. Lucey

While describing the work of the noble and patriotic women of the South during the long and heroic period of four years of Civil war, something would be lacking if we should fail to mention in appropriate terms the good deeds of the Sisters of Mercy. It happened, at the time mentioned, that they were the only Catholic sisterhood in Arkansas, and that their houses at Little Rock, Fort Smith and Helena, though they were strictly literary academies, and though the sisters were trained as teachers only, were freely opened out to the needs of the sick and wounded soldiers, and the services of the sisters given as circumstances demanded. Some of the papers printed will no doubt furnish many interesting details of hospital work at Little Rock, Fort Smith and Helena; and from them some idea may be formed of the opportunities afforded to the Sisters of Mercy to carry into effect their ardent desires. Their visits to the local hospitals in charge of the ladies' associations were always highly appreciated by the patients and the officers in charge.

THEIR WORK IN LITTLE ROCK

The number of sick and wounded soldiers was greater in Little Rock from the very beginning of the war than in any other city of the State. In 1863 there was a notable increase, so that the ordinary Confederate army hospitals were overcrowded. The Sisters of Mercy of St. Mary's Academy fitted up one of their own buildings and received as many as could possibly be allowed entrance. The death rate was great, two or three dying daily. Everything possible for the amelioration of suffering was done. After the capture of the city by General Steele, September 10, 1863, the position of the sisters became almost unbearable, on account of the rude behavior of Federal officers and soldiers, who resented the kind treatment which the Sisters of Mercy were giving to the Confederate sick and wounded. Many years afterward Rev. Mother Alphonsus said to the writer: "We took care of the Confederates and the Federals took care of us."

The retreat of General Sterling Price from his raid in Missouri in September of 1864 also brought many a poor soldier to the care of the Sisters of Mercy. His troops suffered terribly from cold, sickness and exposure. The indefatigable efforts of the sisters to soothe at least the dying agonies of their patients made a profound impression, and several soldiers embraced the Catholic faith, as much perhaps as a testimonial of gratitude to their holy nurses as a conviction of religious truth. Very Rev. Patrick O'Reilly (Father Pat), V. G., from June, 1862, to February, 1867, administrator of the diocese, was the pastor of St. Andrews' cathedral, then the only Catholic church in the city.

The following sisters were members of the community of St. Mary's Academy, Little Rock, Ark., in the period of the Civil war: Mother Alphonsus, Sister M. Xavier, Sister M. Agnes, Sister M. Stanislaus, Sister M. Vincent, Sister Rose, Sister Mary and Sister Michael.

ST. ANNE'S AT FORT SMITH

St. Anne's Academy was located by the Sisters of Mercy, 1851, in the old army headquarters of General Zachary Taylor, just outside the city limits of those times, on an elevated and beautiful site. Their boarding pupils came from the borders of Texas, Indian Territory and several counties of Arkansas. The day pupils from the town and surrounding country homes combined with the boarders to make what was called in those times a large school. The Civil war frightened away the boarders, and in the later stages of it, the greater number of day scholars, also, as parents were chary of risking the absence of their little ones from home. Their fear was all the more intense from the fact that the Indians just across the river were divided into two hostile camps, those under Stand Watie were faithful to the Confederacy while those under Opotheohola fought for the Union. In 1864, John Harrington, a very worthy citizen, was murdered and scalped by the Indians within three miles of Fort Smith.

Another circumstance should be mentioned, not merely that the position of the Sisters of Mercy may be better understood, but also that the noble sacrifices of the women of Fort Smith and the State may be properly estimated. To give the little delicacies to the sick and wounded, generally called for personal privations. It is related that a woman in Richmond, Va., in the last year of the war, when scarcely a cup of tea or coffee could be had for love or money, was entertaining Gen. Robert E. Lee. He came to her house fagged and worn out, to rest an hour or two. She knew his love for a cup of good tea. It happened that there was barely enough to make two cups of tea. She gave Gen. Lee one, and, having deftly filled her own cup with colored water, prevailed on him to take the second cup, which revived his exhausted strength in a wonderful manner. She knew well enough that had he known the facts he would not have taken a second cup. This is a specimen of the work of Southern women. Hundreds of instances could be given.

In those early days there were no railroads. Large side-wheel steamboats traversed the waters of the Arkansas river up as far as Fort Smith. The merchants were accustomed to get six or twelve months' supplies at a time, and every citizen was expected to act accordingly. Steamboats ceased to run after 1861, except as army transports. Some effort was made to obviate the necessity of distant supplies, by home manufacture of leather, salt, breadstuffs and such necessaries, and by the raising of chickens and hogs for meat. All the grains that could be procured, barley, wheat, corn, and also sweet potatoes, were used to obtain a substitute for coffee. But time and trouble rendered almost every substitute a costly and sometimes a dangerous affair for the noble women who visited the hospitals.

In fitting out the soldiers for the campaign of Oak Hill, Elk Horn and Prairie Grove one article was generally a roll of lint bandage for wounds which every soldier was expected to receive. While some of the soldiers, for reasons best known to themselves, preferred the articles that came from the hands of special young ladies, many others thought there was some virtue in the rolls of lint that came from the convent, especially as those contained an inside package of needle and thread.

The time had arrived all too soon when war put on its most serious aspect. When the gay youth and confident soldiers, returning from a campaign, appeared with only the semblance of a uniform. Many were mere boys, and when they appeared before the Sisters of Mercy wrapped in tatters and rags, without shoes and with only a show of a hat, the sight was enough to move any woman's heart. The barn and other habitable outhouses of the convent were utilized as sanitariums. while food and clothing were being prepared. In a week or two these soldiers would feel strong enough to join their command, but the rustic sanitarium seemed to be always well patronized. The soldiers who were thus benefitted were frequently reminded of their own homes by the kindly sympathy of the sisters. That womanly influence which brightens so many homes and softens the stronger ways of men, had been so long absent from the lives of the soldiers, that one or two weeks spent in the company of the Sisters of Mercy seemed to restore the equilibrium of their existence.

AIDED WOUNDED OF BOTH ARMIES

The day of the battle of Fort Smith, August 24, 1864, when General Cooper attempted to drive the Federal commander, General Curtis, from the town, brought great excitement to the convent. A guard of soldiers had been sent in the morning to all the churches and as, the men came out they were marched out to the trenches and put to work throwing up fortifications. In the attacking army of Confederates were many of the sons and relations of the men working that Sunday on Federal fortifications. General Cooper was repulsed. Then the work of the Sisters of Mercy began in earnest for the care of the wounded. While their personal sympathies were naturally in favor of the South, their vows of religion led them to treat with every possible kindness the Federal sick and wounded. The Confederates held Fort Smith until 1863, when General Blunt captured it without a battle, outflanking with a superior force General W. L. Cabell. What the Sisters of Mercy had done under Confederate occupation, they continued to do under Federal rule. It is well to state that neither Confederate nor Federal soldiers ever offered any indignity to the Sisters of Mercy in any part of the state. An occasional guard of soldiers would be sent to protect their property. At Little Rock General Steele maintained a guard at the convent for seventeen months.

GIANT TROOPER CAUSED PANIC

The convent of Fort Smith was situated in a beautiful grove and only separated by a roadway from the larger grove where the church and pastor's house were located. The Confederate army had always respected the rights of church and sisters, so that the groves had not been used as a camp ground. Quantrell, the noted guerrilla chieftain, arrived at Fort Smith in 1863 with a squadron of 200 cavalry. The men wore the regulation blue of the Union army, heavy overcoats, hats and boots. As they generally captured a Federal train every month or two, their dress was spic and span. As for arms, they were literally loaded with them. A rifle was slung over the shoulder, a heavy navy revolver was belted on either side, a good sized knife showed itself, and a sabre completed the accoutrement. They pitched camp in the grove opposite the convent and within a few minutes one of the troopers stood in the doorway of the school. The boys and girls had studied mythology and had read about giants, so that when they looked up from their books and caught sight of Quantrell's trooper he seemed to be at least ten feet high, and with overcoat enough to carry them all away. They sprang through the windows in every direction and made their way to the town, where they reported that Quantrell's men were pillaging the convent. A prominent Catholic of the town, father of the writer of this paper, who knew Quantrell, hailed him as he was riding by and told him the news. Quantrell said that such an affair was not his style of business and immediately dispatched an officer to look into the matter. The trooper in coming to the school wanted merely a chunk of burning wood to start the camp fire. Matches were too precious to be used except in cases of extreme necessity. Quantrell was a mild-mannered man in his intercourse with people. His medium height and fair complexion, with reddish hair and beard, would not indicate the extraordinary bravery which be exhibited in time of battle, nor anything of that terrible retaliation which followed the extraordinary outrages which he and many of his men had endured in Kansas and Missouri.

Very Reverend Lawrence Smythe, V. F., was the pastor at Fort Smith from 1861 to the end of the war. The following sisters were members of the community of St. Anne's academy from 1861 to 1865:

Sisters M. Baptist, John, Magdalene, Vincentia and De Sales.

THE WORK IN HELENA

The Sisters of Mercy had acquired in the late fifties the beautiful residence of the Biscoe family, adjoining that of General Hindman and General Cleburne, for their convent and school. Rev. Philip Shanahan was the pastor. Rt. Rev. Andrew Byrne, the first Catholic bishop in Arkansas, died there June 18, 1862.

The hospital work of the sisters was much the same in Helena as in Fort Smith and Little Rock. It was subjected to much irregularity on account of the delay in establishing any general system of hospital work. The medical staff was at all times less in numbers and in suitable equipment than even necessity required. This is why the ladies of the different cities and the Sisters of Mercy were almost always thrown upon their own individual resources. This will also explain why few exact reports can be made of much of the work.

It is said that disease kills more soldiers than battles. Helena was at all times a military center and the hospitals never closed their doors. When General Holmes made a furious attack on Helena July 4, 1863, then held by General Curtis, the Union commander, the Sisters of Mercy from their elevated convent were able to see the battle raging in all its fury. They saw the standard-bearer in an advanced position fall to the ground, trailing the banner of the South, and, in spite of their prayers, they saw victory go down with the stars and bars.

> "Where before the altar hung
> The proud banner, which with prayer,
> Had been consecrated there;
> And the nuns' sweet hymns were heard the while,
> Sung low in the dim, mysterious aisle."

The repulse of General Holmes is said to have weighed heavily on his mind for many years. He was sure of victory and looked upon his plans as perfect. Within a few hours after the close of the battle the Sisters of Mercy turned their St. Catherine's Academy into both a morgue and a hospital. They helped to coffin many a poor soldier, if a rough box could be styled a coffin. The wounded in all stages of suffering demanded immediate attention. Those only who have visited a battle field after an engagement can understand what the good ladies of Helena and the Sisters of Mercy were obliged to endure in the performance of hospital work.

In conclusion it may be truly said that as great as the work of the women of the South was in the tumult of war, a large share of the responsibilities consequent of the result of the long contest fell to them in the care of the widow and orphan. The Confederacy was filled with children without father or mother and it is well known to those who are familiar with the life of the institutions under charge of the Sisters of Mercy, that many a child was reared to a high and happy career through their noble charity.

---------------ᴏᏚ₃·ᏋᏚᏗ---------------

FEDERAL RAIDERS OF MISSISSIPPI
By Mrs. Mary Brunson, of Little Rock

Although I am now and have been for many years a resident of Arkansas, the incidents that I narrate occurred at the old family home near Byhalia, Miss. My father, C. N. Stevens, and my two brothers, William Stevens and James Bailey, were Confederate soldiers.

RAID BY YANKEE SOLDIERS

The women of the house had been spinning yarn and weaving cloth very quietly until they were able to make two suits of gray, two soldiers' caps, and two pairs of soldiers' boots. These were precious articles. We personally placed them upstairs in a barrel with a lot of old rags filled in on top. We had reason to believe that if the Yankees found them the things would be lost and our house burned. The Yank raiding party came as we feared they would, but failed to find our barrel. They found many other things; in fact, looted the house, and having compelled my mother to cook almost everything edible in the house, left with all our stock. We grieved especially over the loss of our family horse and buggy mule. As all our neighbors suffered in like manner, however, we had no special reason to complain.

THE FATHER REPORTED KILLED

We were most cruelly distressed by the news that father had been killed, but later on we learned he was in Memphis in the Irvin block, a prisoner. Dr. Miller of Cocrum, Miss., was with him. They had passed themselves off as citizens, but every moment feared that some one would recognize them. In three months they managed to get paroled. Father returned home and for a time all our sorrows were forgotten.

COTTON $1 A POUND

When the Southern army was obliged to retreat it frequently happened that quantities of cotton had been accumulated to ship to Europe, and when it was seen that it would all fall into the hands of the enemy, the Confederate general would order it to be burned. Everybody would try to hide what they could. My mother had saved some cotton belonging to my brother, James, which she had stored in an outhouse and covered with fodder. This was saved, and she sold it for $70 in gold, which she buried, and when my brother came home she gave it to him. The blockades, general and local, of those times made it very difficult to procure the necessaries of life, even with gold. In 1865 flour was $17 a barrel and salt was $50 a barrel.

RAID OF CLAYTON'S REGIMENT
By Mrs. S. D. Dickon, of Lockesburg

I noticed a statement in the Lockesburg Enterprise where the women of Arkansas were invited to write and tell how they suffered in the war of '61-'65. I could not write you all I did suffer when Col. Clayton, the Northern man, was at Pine Bluff, He sent his men to make raids on the Southerners and destroy all they could, besides taking everything of value for themselves. The first thing they started out to do was to take everything they could find. Twenty bales of cotton were taken out of the smokehouse at one time, five horses were also taken. They searched the house and got every article of any value they could find. Sometimes it would take one and a half days for us to get any food.

We had three large barns full of corn. Twenty wagons were sent at a time and nearly all the corn taken. My husband, was in the Confederate army and I was left with two little children to care for. Two thousand pounds of meat were taken from us and my life threatened if the key of my trunk was not delivered to them. Clayton's men went down in our pasture, and all the beeves were killed and taken away. I could not rest at night for being uneasy about my husband, and for fear they would kill us or burn our house down. Our slaves made all they could on the farm with hoes for we had no horses. I worked in the field myself with my children following me.

One time the Federals overtook the slaves hauling cotton from the gin, and it was taken from them. My husband died in '81 and I was left penniless with five children. The Federals broke us up and after the war my husband was only an invalid, and I had harder times than during the war. I am now 64 years old and am penniless as I was then. I cannot work much. Well, I will stop at this point as I could not tell it all anyway.

———————— ම&ඁ-ළ-ෂ@————————

THE DAUGHTER OF THE FIRST ARKANSAS REGIMENT
By *Miss Laura Govan, of Marianna*

The subject of this sketch, Mrs. Charles Richard Cockle, is the eldest daughter of the late Major General James F. Fagan, of Arkansas. She has the proud distinction of bearing the title of "Daughter of the First Arkansas Regiment," having been so christened and adopted by the regiment while it was encamped at Brook's Station, Virginia, in 1861, the regiment having, immediately upon its organization left, under command of General (then Colonel) Fagan, for Virginia, Mrs. Fagan with her two children accompanying her husband.

The adoption occurred at time of dress parade, the regimental ceremony of the day, the companies in their best attire, the officers in full dress, guns burnished, bayonets gleaming in the sunlight, the sound of music's martial strains caught up in the soft spring air and wafted across Virginia's hills, and over all floated the folds of the Southern flag, as yet unriddled by shot or shell. Mrs. Cockle was at that time four years of age; her dress was typical of the inherited instincts of the soldier which have characterized her whole life, red pants, a white blouse with embroidered ruffle at neck and wrists; over this a Zouave jacket of red, the small three-cornered hat of the same bright, warm hue, with ribbon rosettes bearing the colors of the Southern standard. The address of adoption was delivered on behalf of the regiment by the Adjutant, who was afterwards Major Bronaugh, commanding a battalion of the troops. Rev. R. W. Trimble, chaplain of the regiment, christened the little Irene, "Daughter of the First Arkansas Regiment."

The touching and beautiful incident is a part of the lost cause, and has lived in the hearts of the veterans, witness their tribute to their "Daughter," so touchingly bestowed only a short time ago, when the regimental flag, the precious relic which has been so tenderly, reverently preserved through all the years, was presented to her by the veterans of the Confederate camp at Newport, Ark. To insure the preservation of the treasure, Mrs. Cockle has since presented it to the Confederate Museum at Richmond, Virginia.

During a visit to her sister, Mrs. Watson, in Newport, Mrs. Cockle was given a reception by the loyal daughters of Arkansas, who, through her, paid tribute to her father. Arkansas' illustrious son, Colonel Minor, in behalf of the "Daughters," presented Mrs. Cockle a little flag, with the following touching remarks: "As the 'daughter of the First Arkansas Regiment,' we do you but slight honor in this impromptu affair. Your gallant father led this flag in many a deadly battle, honored it and loved it until the day of his death, in peace; but bowed ever with submission to the inevitable when the conditions so required. In behalf of the Daughters of the Lucian C. Gause Chapter, I present you with this slight token of the renewed love of those of the First

Arkansas Regiment who are left behind for the time being, and yet cherish the love that was close and sweet in
the sixties, hoping that you have in no wise diminished
in the faith you imbibed in those days, but will hold to
your children's children and their generations the old
love for the South, and that the Confederacy will, in the
memory of all, live forever."

Mrs. Cockle was the guest of the veterans of Fagan
Camp at Barren Fork, Ark., in the fall of 1905. A parade of the veterans through the little town, and a service at the church, were features of the welcome and
abundant hospitality accorded the daughter of their old
comrade. The occasion was replete with reminiscences
of valiant deeds in the heroic struggle for the right, and
pictures of the past would grow, "soldiers of the Confederacy," standing as they might have stood on the eve
of battle, some summer day in the early sixties, in long
trim lines, silk and gold above them, and the green hills
of Virginia stretching away behind; the pictures would
give way, and in their stead with youthful, eager, boyish
faces; with the flashing of flags would appear the reality
of the hour, the veterans sitting there listening to
"The tales that will not die."

---------🙰🙰---------

SKETCH OF MRS. W. F. SLEMMONS
By Mrs. Willie Slemmons Duke, of Monticello

My mother, Mrs. W. F. Slemmons, often speaks of
her first experience with "the Yankees," as most
thrilling. Being the wife of an officer, (Colonel in 2nd

Arkansas Cavalry), she had more to contend with than did her neighbors. Like all other Southern women, she had talked of and dreaded the coming of the "blue coats," but when they did come, it was quite an unpleasant surprise. My father had just gotten home from a long campaign in Mississippi, the night before, and that morning after being assured by his scouts that there were no Federals in this vicinity he went into town to transact some business. About 11 o'clock, the faithful negro girl "Beck" called from the back yard, "Lawsy, Miss Marthy, de soldiers is comin'," and on looking out my mother saw the soldiers, and also saw that they wore the blue. Her first thought was of her little children playing in a nearby grove, so charging Beck to hide the colonel's belongings, she rushed out, but was halted at the gate, but was finally permitted to go on. When she returned with the frightened babies clinging to her, she found that her house had been searched from top to bottom, but they had found no trace of my father, as Beck with the native cunning of her race, had not only concealed everything belonging to him, but had told the soldiers such clever stories of "not 'spectin' Marse Williams for two or three days," that they went away, taking with them three valuable horses.

Late in the afternoon she received the welcome news that Col. Slemmons was, safe at his father's home, three miles from town. He had been hidden in the loft of the Jones' hotel when the soldiers passed through town. On leaving town afoot, he fortunately met my grandmother Howard on her favorite horse, Pompey. On learning his plight she dismounted at once and gave him her horse on which mount he proceeded to Louisiana to join Gen. Kirby Smith. When my mother began to pack up his clothing to send to him, she found that Beck had hidden his uniform in a feather bed. Needless to say it was in a sad condition. The next day the same brigade commanded by Major McCauley came back, and on learning in town how they had been duped in regard to Col. Slemmons' whereabouts, they came to the house, took everything they could carry—silver, dishes, provisions, even the dinner cooking on the stove, which they gave to a wagonload of negroes who were going with them. Finding the carefully hoarded stock of sugar and meal too heavy, they scattered it along the road. They tried in vain to induce the faithful Beck to join them, but she rejected their offers of freedom, money, etc., with fine scorn. In a final burst of rage they poured a bottle of turpentine in the hall, and set fire to, it, then departed, but with only the assistance of the negro girl, mother fought the flames, and quenched the fire before any great damage was done. Major McCauley was not with his men at the time and came later to apologize for their vandalism. As he left he said: "Tell Col. Slemmons to come up and surrender like a little man. I'll be glad to see him and treat him right." Mother replied that perhaps when the meeting took place he wouldn't be so glad, and this proved true, for only a short time after the Major was captured at the battle of Mark's Mill and on learning who his captor was, said, "Well, Colonel, I'm not half as glad to see you as I thought I'd be when I sent a message to you by your wife."

———————⊗⅋ɜ·ε·ꙅ⊛———————

SUFFERINGS OF ELLIS FAMILY AT
BAILEY SPRINGS, ALA.
By Mrs. Cora Williamson Rodgers, of Nashville

My grandfather, Albert Gallatin Ellis, a proud son of
Virginia, and my grandmother, Mary Llewellyn
Hewlett Ellis, owned and resided at Bailey Springs,
Ala., a summer resort, nine miles from Florence, a
thriving town. Their son, William P., a lad at college,
two daughters, Virginia and Mattie, and a grandson, six
or seven years old, comprised the family. My grandfather being too old for active military service and feeble
in health, besides, could be at home very little on account of the villainous tories, who persecuted him and
all other reputable Southerners. When the Yankee invaders came they soon decided that Bailey Springs with
its ample buildings and grounds was an ideal place for
winter quarters and rendezvous generally. Here they
would camp for months at a time.

The officers were usually well behaved, though the
privates were thieving, impudent and often tyrannical,
plundering and pillaging everything that could be
found. The cattle, farm stock and sometimes the slaves
were sent some distance across Shoal Creek for safe
keeping. The supplies, hogshead of sugar, molasses,
etc., were rolled under the house, which was high at
one end and then covered with brush and rubbish.

The jewelry, silver and such valuables were hid
numbers of times and at last, Jennie, the daughter, a
nervous girl, hurriedly buried the jewelry on approach
of the Yankees and in her fright could never remember
where. It was never found unless the raiders got it.

A large number of faithful slaves, houses, land and stock, were to be looked after and cared for. Grandmother and her daughters managed all this, besides always finding time to sew, knit and look after our "dear boys in gray," of which they never tired. Many a wounded soldier sick and discouraged found succor under their hospitable roof, and was sent away well and happy, ready to enter the service again. The tories and bushwhackers often committed the most horrible crimes. Avoiding the war they sneaked about to persecute those who were left at home, women, children and feeble and aged men, robbing and destroying on every hand. The little grandson, Willie A. Ellis, was sent every few days to a settlement three miles distant to learn the news and the movements of the two armies. Mr. Wilson a wealthy gentleman, lived there with two small nephews. One morning Willie was sent as usual for news and on his return related that Mr. Wilson had been murdered and burned by the Yankees. He was sick in bed when the Yankees asked where his money was and on his failure to produce it piled papers saturated with turpentine on him and set it on fire, burning the old man to death; killing one nephew, wounding the other who rolled under the bed and escaped to tell the awful tale. His slaves all fled and the whole country was horror-stricken at the enormity of this crime. Many were afraid to have burning light at night and some hid themselves away until they felt the danger over. These heinous crimes were often committed and caused continual fear and consternation among the women and children. Oh, the agony of the poor women and children and the infirm men, they never knew at what moment they might be pounced upon and sacrificed. Their helplessness was most pathetic, and oftentimes they were even afraid to get out and bury their holy dead. How I wish a full history of the war in the South, its depreciations, desecrations and destruction both of holy and unholy things could be had. The history of the Turkish and Armenian war would pale into nothingness beside it, since they are unchristian and little better is expected of them. At one time a number of Yankees came and appropriated my grandmother's breakfast as fast and as often as the cook could prepare it.

Finally, the daughter, Mattie, a plucky girl, decided she should have her breakfast and stood guard while it was being cooked. When it was again ready a Yank was on hand, ready also and reaching his hand to help himself when Mattie flourished a stick of stove-wood and said, "touch if you dare." The man drew back and skipped out, pretending to be much frightened, he was cowed because of the cowardly trick. The whole country was beseiged by Yankees and picketed so as to prevent passing, buying or selling, and often supplies would run short. Oftentimes rye, barley and potatoes would be parched and a concoction made of it to imitate coffee, no doubt a poor imitation, but better than none. Shoes and gloves were made at home from skins of animals killed at home, the tallow candle, and those of beeswax and resin supplied the light after coal oil gave out. These were the arc lights of the war.

My grandfather continued to grow worse and at last succumbed to heart disease in 1864. I think grandmother survived him many years. Two daughters, Mary Ellis Williamson and Mattie Ellis Caruthers and William P. Ellis are still enjoying a lonely old age, and William A. Ellis, the grandson, is now a middle-aged father and husband. There are living, eighteen grandchildren, and seventeen great-grandchildren from this grand old couple. May they all live to honor and glorify their ancestors as they should be honored and glorified.

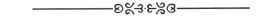

ARKANSAS WOMAN CAPTURED BY A GUNBOAT

Mrs. Samuel Gondelock, of Union District, went West with her husband just prior to the war. He was killed in Arkansas while serving with the Western army of the Confederacy, and with her two little girls the mother attempted to get back from Arkansas to South Carolina. The Mississippi River was then patrolled by Federal gunboats and as she was being rowed across she was espied and stopped, brought aboard a gunboat and her trunks opened and contents examined. Nothing incriminating being found she was landed on the Eastern bank and finally reached home.

J. L. Strain.

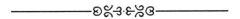

THE WILLIAMSON FAMILY OF ALABAMA
By Mrs. Cora Williamson Rodgers, of Nashville

My father, Capt. Samuel Zachariah Williamson and his wife, Mary H. Ellis Williamson were but recently married, when my father was called to the front. He soon became Captain of 2nd Mississippi Partizans, serving till the close of the war, leaving my mother and her twin babies, and a small son of a former wife, in the care of God and the faithful slaves. The negroes made the crop and protected the little family as best they could.

My mother had mortal fear of the enemy, who robbed, pillaged and destroyed every available thing. At one time they carried off all the provisions on the place, and when she told them there was nothing left for them to eat, one of the insolent creatures turned and threw her a package and told her she could keep that. It proved to be a bundle of spice, which is good in its place but a poor substitute for bread. They drove my father's handsome carriage and high-bred horses to the door and loaded it with books from a splendid library. These they had no use for, but scattered and destroyed them most wantonly. Years afterwards my father had a letter from someone saying, he had found his name in a book on the parlor table in the house of a man living in Michigan. It was never recovered however. Their jewelry and silverware was sent down to a friend's in the river bottom, who kept them until the terrible days were over. But my mother's fine dresses and in fact, everything else were carried away by raiders and thieves.

Once my father, on arriving home from the battles, heard of a woman who had some smuggled coffee in the neighborhood. He remounted his horse and rode for hours to overtake her and buy some, even a little, for be it remembered, that coffee, sugar, provisions and medicines were not allowed by the Yankees to be sold to Southerners, who had possession of Memphis, and the Yankees were trying to starve them into surrender. Provisions and medicines, especially quinine and whiskey, were often smuggled by the women, for the lives of the Southern soldiers often depended on these two articles. Sometimes medicines were sewed in the lining of their dresses. Spinning, weaving and knitting occupied the time of most Southern women, preparing boxes of clothing, medicine, provisions to be sent with words of cheer. During this time another son was born to them and death claimed their twin boys, one only a few hours after the other. My mother's delicate health and nature almost succumbed to this terrible shock, which required more fortitude than any one can ever understand, being separated from parents and husband, with raiders appearing at any moment. Kind friends and dear hands constructed a nice walnut coffin, covered it with velvet, a luxury at that time, and the little ones were consigned to mother earth, clasped in the arms of one another, as they entered this world. My father surrendered at Gainesville, Ala., and as the railroad wires were torn up by Yanks, came home on a hand car with others who took turn about, walking to push, often mending the broken railroad to continue their journey. His negroes were free, he was without a dollar, disheartened, almost heartbroken over the sad fall of the brave South, but like the hero he was, he took his small son and tried to farm. His negroes, however, soon decided he was the best master to be found, and nearly all returned to work for him, and helped him to regain his fortune. Both parents still live in the old home at Sardis, Miss., and would be glad to hear from any old friend or comrade in those squally times. They live to recount the incidents of the war, and many, many hours have I sat at my fathers knee, listening and never tiring of listening to the brave deeds, narrow escapes, trying times, hardships, such as sleeping on two rails in a fence corner, and thought the rails a great luxury. The stories of the thirst and hunger so often suffered by him and his comrades was to me simply terrible. At that time money was scarce and worth little. Calico was a dollar a yard. Spool thread a dollar. Shoes ten dollars to seventy-five dollars. Flannel that first wrapped my husband cost seventy-five dollars a yard. His first shoes cost one hundred dollars—quite a big sum for baby shoes.

But those trying times are past, may they never return. When Christianity burns in every heart as it should, wars, tumults and strife of all kinds will end.

SKETCH OF MRS. LAURA C. DOSWELL, OF NEWPORT
By Mrs. C. H. Wilmans, of Newport

Mrs. Laura C. Doswell, of Newport, Ark., is one of the true type of loyal Southern women. She came to Arkansas from Virginia, to make her home out here with her brother, Colonel Franklin Doswell, many years ago. Mrs. Doswell's experiences as a young girl, during the war between the States, are very interesting and quite worthy of place in the historical pamphlet, but her extreme modesty prevents our securing a very extensive account of the subject.

One interesting experience of Mrs. Doswell is told most entertainingly by her, in about these words, "Yes, I remember so clearly the sad day on which the battle of Manassas was fought. Sunday, July 21. I was at Old Fork church that day. As soon as possible, several from our neighborhood, myself among the number, went to Culpepper Court House, to assist in caring for the dead and dying men there. We took with us many dainties, medicines, and all sorts of supplies. A hospital had been temporarily established at a large private residence. I was stationed in the linen room there, where I remained for many weeks assisting in getting ready the clothes, bed linens, bandages, etc., for the wounded and dying. The lady in charge of this department was Mrs. Dade, the widow of Major Dade, killed in the Seminole war in Florida. O! child, there are so many painful recollections! But my service was so little and my experiences like those of so many others." And thus it is we fail to get lengthy articles from these brave and modest women. When we read between the lines we can not fail to see the suffering and sacrifices, the sacredness of sorrow that neither they nor we can put into words.

Mrs. Doswell sends a contribution of money, saying that she desires "to assist in building the monument to those noble women who so deserve it." She does not seem to realize the fact, but nevertheless she is truly one of "those noble women."

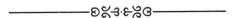

CRUELTIES OF 13TH KANSAS CAVALRY
By Mrs. Jeffers, of Ozark

My husband, Daniel Jeffers, was three years in the Confederate army. He left me with two small children on a farm near Mulberry. The place was some distance from a neighbor's house and many a time I gazed in silence on the sleeping forms of my babes and wondered

how long I should be obliged to live that lonely life and
how long I should dread to hear a gun go off, as it made
me think of my husband on the battlefield far away, indeed, but so easily recalled.

BREAKS A YOUNG HORSE

There was no income from the farm and no way to
get anything from it except I worked it myself. I plowed
in the field day after day. I broke a young horse to the
plow that a fifteen-year-old boy had failed to make
work. The hardships endured in these long years can
only be understood by women who went through similar experiences. Now and then, as strength began to fail
me, kind neighbors would lend a hand and my husband's little brother and my own would help me over
the worst work.

CRUELTIES OF BUSHWHACKERS

The retreat of Gen. T. C. Hindman after the battle of
Prairie Grove left our section full of marauders of all
kinds, chiefly Federal soldiers and bushwhackers. Small
bands of these inhuman wretches came to our homes
and tortured old men and women by applying burning
wood and hot coals to the soles of their feet until they
told where money and other valuables were hidden.
Many times when there was nothing hidden away and
at others when some old man or woman would not tell
where treasure was secreted, many cruelties were practiced. In a neighbor's house these villains poured hot
coals down a lady's back because she was unwilling or
unable to satisfy their demands. The mental horrors and

apprehensions which such outrages created in every woman's mind that heard of them were among our most dreaded trials in those times.

FEDERAL SCOUTS EAT LAST MORSEL

Many a time these raiders would dash up to my house, search under the beds and in every closet and place where I tried to hide bread and meat for myself and little ones, and then compel me with oaths and indecent language to prepare a lavish meal out of my very scanty food. I thought in those days that I could never bring myself to look upon a Federal soldier with anything but disgust and hatred, as the cruelties of the Thirteenth Kansas, who wore that blue, were villainous.

HUSBAND REPORTED KILLED

My husband got a brief furlough one time and made his way home. A scouting party of the Thirteenth Kansas rushed upon my house and told me that they had killed him in the woods near by. The horrors of those hours will never be forgotten. About 9 o'clock that night I heard the sound of my husband's voice in the chimney corner outside, asking me to bring him something to eat. He was afraid to enter the house, as the scouts were camped a half mile away and some might be watching. Some time previously I had hidden a little corn, wheat and meat on a bluff, but the scouting thieves found my store, but before they could take it all away I managed a day or two before the last raid to bring some of it home. The Thirteenth Kansas now came and took everything except a small piece of meat.

After their departure I picked up a peck of corn from the floor, which they had spilled and tramped over.

RODE 40 MILES TO VISIT HUSBAND

Through one of those circumstances that frequently befell the Southern soldier and family within the enemy's lines, my husband was captured. From a reliable source I learned that he was in the guard house at Van Buren, 40 miles away. I saddled my poor old pony, and, placing my babe in my lap, started on the journey, as I could not rest after hearing the news. Those who have traveled in that part of the country know how many streams there are to cross and they were all swollen at that time. Big Mulberry and Little Mulberry were very high. I was very tired and worn when I reached Van Buren, but went direct to the headquarters of the colonel commanding the post. No sooner did I mention my business to this officer than he used ungentlemanly and abusive language and turned his back upon me. He did not seem to have a spark of human sympathy in his breast. With my tired body and blighted hopes I went away with streaming eyes, having no one to call on for comfort except "Him who doeth all things well." After many rebuffs and on a promise to leave for home on the morrow, I got permission to spend the night with my husband in the guard house. Next morning I was compelled to start on my homeward journey, not having accomplished anything, heart heavy and sick in soul and body. I thought that I would never see my husband again in this world. But our heavenly Father does more for us than we should expect. The very next night my husband escaped from prison and reached home before me and baby.

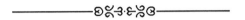

EXPERIENCES OF MRS. J. S. ADAMSON *

When the Civil War broke out we were living in Pine Bluff. My father was too old to respond to the first call for volunteers. On the second call he offered his services and was assigned to the Commissary Department, serving until the Confederate Army left Pine Bluff for the southern part of the State. My father being in wretched health at that time, was advised by Gen. Roane (formerly Gov. Roane), to remain at home. He was given an honorable discharge with his little pay in the shape of a hogshead of sugar, the Confederates at that time having more sugar than greenbacks.

The Yankees arrived in a few days with flashing sabers and big oaths. Fortunately for our family, the commander in charge, Gen. Powell Clayton, took up his headquarters across the street from us. This afforded us some protection because the soldiers were afraid to commit any depradations so close to headquarters. After I got over my scare of the Yankees I would ride a few blocks every day until I was ordered by the Yankees to stay in the yard.

In a short time the rumor got out that my father was in communication with the Southern soldiers, and to make things worse for us, the Confederates surprised

---

* This account did not appear in the original edition, but was printed in the minutes of the U. D. C. Convention.

the Yankees one beautiful Sabbath morning, coming in
on our side of town. The citizens were ordered under
the river bank. My mother had been sick for several
weeks and was too ill to be moved, and of course we
could not leave her. We piled feather beds on her to
protect her as much as possible from the bullets which
were peppering the house like hail. The Confederates
charged down the streets, the Yankees giving way all
the time until they got their breastworks thrown up,
then they made a stand. I heard the commander of the
Confederates shout, "Take the houses on them, boys."
As the Yankees had their batteries turned on them, and
were firing up the street, a lot of Confederates fired
from our porch. They fought for several hours; the
Confederates had to retreat. I have not time to tell you
what we suffered after this battle. We were then ordered out of the lines. We had no place to go. My father
went to Gen. Clayton, told him we had a few things we
would like to take out of the lines with us, and told him
about the sugar. Gen. Clayton said he would give him a
pass, and if he could get it through, all right. Well, a
good faithful negro servant fixed that sugar in barrels,
tied old meal sacks over them and smeared soft soap on
the sacks, and when they were loading it she would call
out not to spill her soap.

Mrs. Sam Roane came to our rescue and gave us a
home on her plantation several miles from Pine Bluff. It
was in the fall of 1863 that we moved to this place. It
was very dangerous in this part of the country. Our
nearest neighbor was Col. Embry, a brother of Mrs.
Roane, who lived two miles away.

He was quite an old gentleman. I have heard him
say that the Jayhawkers kept a rope around his neck so

much that he didn't need a collar. I know it is unnecessary to explain to people who lived in war time that the term "Jayhawker" was applied to a class of men who fought with neither army, but robbed and imposed on helpless men, women and children. Mrs. Roane rented her place to a couple of New York men who were neutral; that is, didn't take sides with either party. They employed my father to teach their overseers how to raise cotton. The negroes would not let "that old Rebel," as they called my father, come in the field; he would give his instructions in the house.

The Jayhawkers soon began to make raids on these men and they finally went to Gen. Clayton and got a negro guard. My father did not know of this until they marched a negro company on the place; then he told them they had made a mistake, that he wouldn't remain on the place with negro soldiers. They had only been there a few days when a company of Confederates dashed in and shot everything they saw with blue clothes on. My father had 30,000 bushels of corn in a large building on the river ready to ship. He had ridden up there to meet a boat when these men dashed up and came straight to the house. My mother, sister and myself were alone. All the negroes that were in the quarters rushed to the house for protection. The negro men who wore blue clothes were shot in our yard. The Rebels divided and part of them dashed through the fields toward the river, and in a few moments we saw flames shooting out of the house where the corn was stored. My mother said, "Run, Bettie, they are burning your father." Of course she was crazed with fright. I tried to catch my pony but he was almost scared to death by the shouts, firing and the screams. I started on a run through the field; it was about a mile to the river. The Confederates had finished their work at the house and came rushing through the field to the fire, which was something dreadful to witness. They called to me as they dashed by to go back home, but I was deaf to their advice; I feld sure that my father had been killed by the negroes. When I got about half way to the house that was burning, I looked back and saw two negro soldiers riding toward me. They were heavily armed, and they came right on. When the Confederates spied them they came on a sweeping gallop to meet them. They saw they were lost and rushed toward me, jumped off the mules, threw down their guns, and grabbed me for protection. The soldiers dashed up and shot these two negroes dead while they were holding on to me. Fully twenty shots were fired. The smoke was so dense I could not see. The first thing I heard was my father praying to them not to kill his child. He jumped off his horse, ran to me, grabbed me in his arms and cried and begged me to speak to him. I was almost paralyzed with fright. I shall never forget those vise-like black arms that were clinging to me for protection. One of the soldiers lifted me to my father's arms on the horse, more dead than alive. However, I soon rallied when I saw my poor mother needed my attention.

After this fight my father got a permit to move just inside the Yankee pickets. Several weeks after we moved, Col. Embry came to see us, and asked me if I would not like to go to Pine Bluff with him and Mag, his daughter. He said Mrs. Roane had gotten us a pass. I was glad to go, so the following day in the morning, he and Mag came for me. Mrs. Roane had a room at Col. Bell's home in Pine Bluff, the rest of the house being occupied by Federal officers. We spent the night in Mrs. Roane's room, and the next morning we were up early and ready to return home. Mrs. Roane asked me if I would smuggle some things out for her. I said, "If you think I can get them through the lines, I am more than willing." She then told me that Israel Embry, Col. Embry's son, was a Southern soldier, was hid on his father's place and was sick and nearly naked. She asked me if I could help them get a pair of boots, a navy six pistol and ten yards of gray jeans out to him. I agreed to try. Mrs. Roane and Mag put the things on me while Col. Embry watched the enemy. We wore hoopskirts in those days, which made it easy to hide things. The boots were fastened to my hoops and fell between my knees. The pistol was fixed so it lay in my lap. We also wore bustles, which was an excellent place to hide things. I burned my bustle and made one of part of the jeans, tied a string around my waist, run it through the folds of the goods and let it hang down so I could sit on part of it. I wore a heavy riding skirt which helped to conceal the things. Col. Embry led the horses up to the back door. We all mounted at the same time; there was not a Yankee in sight. Just then it was early and they were all asleep. Mrs. Roane bid us all goodby as she was to leave for the south soon after we left. To be shielded as much as possible, I rode between Mag and the Colonel down the street. Everything went well until we got to the Pontoon Bridge across the river. We had agreed that I should ride on ahead, as my pony was already restless, while Col. Embry paid the toll. I was getting along beautifully when all of a sudden a puff of wind struck that pontoon, and it began to swing. My pony got frightened, stood up on his hind feet, cutting all kinds of capers in the middle of the river. I expected every moment to go overboard. Pontoon bridges have no railings, they are only flat boats fastened together. The Yankees on the bank called to me to jump but I stayed in the saddle and tried to quiet my horse and finally succeeded. My horse had attracted so much attention that I felt sure I was caught. A big Yankee came out and took hold of my bridle and led me to an officer. He said, "Cap, we have caught this little Rebel red-handed." The Captain told one of his men to help me down. "No, No," I said, "don't you touch me." I will get down Captain, and give you my word of honor, I will take off all these things I am smuggling if you will make those Yankees keep their hands off." He laughed and said: "All right, go in that tent and be in a hurry, I assure you." When I came out of the tent they all rushed in and the first words the Captain said was, "Good Lord, we have got to fight these Rebels from the cradle up." I was vey indignant at this, for I thought I was of great importance. The Captain turned to me and said, "Do you see that gallows?" Of course I could see it; three or four weeks before that they had hung a young Southern soldier on it, and left the gallows as a warning to others. He said, "You will be next." They put us under a guard and took me to the provost marshal's office. There I found Mag Embry; her father had been put in the guard house. The Yankees made Mag and me take the oath of allegiance. Then, with two soldiers guarding us, we were marched up the street to the place we started from, Col. Bell's residence.

Mrs. Roane had gone for the south two or three hours, when we got there. We were locked up in Mrs. Roane's room with three other girls who were prisoners. Among them was a spy who had been tried for her life, but was not convicted. The next morning two of the girls were set free, but Mag and I were kept under guard for three days. Gen. Clayton sent for my father and told him if he did not make me tell who put those things on me he would imprison us both, and it would go hard with us. The Yankees had released Mag Embry and her father and I was left with the spy. A guard brought my father to me and he said, "Bettie, who put those things on you?" I refused to tell. Then he took me by my shoulders, shook me, and in an angry voice said, "You have to tell; my life depends upon your confession." I knew my father was under suspicion, and that it was no idle threat. This was too much for a girl of 15 years old to bear. The eminent danger to my father left me no alternative but to confess. As Mrs. Roane was far out of danger, I knew that no harm could reach her, so I admitted that she placed the things on me.

Gen. Clayton gave orders to have my pony turned over to me and then told my father to take me home and lock me up. He said that the second offense would be a serious thing. My father only exacted a promise of me not to do anything that would give the Yankees an excuse to punish us. Thus I was compelled to surrender several months before the war was over.

———————————⊗⅌⅗·ℰ⅗⊙———————————

HEROISM OF MRS. N. J. MORTON STAPLES, OF PRAIRIE GROVE

By Mrs. D. H. Torbett

Our Chapter is honored by numbering among its members several women who lived in this, Washington County, Arkansas, during the war between the states, and no one suffered more than they. For the most part they were women who stayed at home and cared for their families as best they could, fed, sewed for and aided the soldiers.

One of these grand old women was Mrs. N. J. Morton Staples. Her home was on the dividing line between the armies of the North and South when the battle of Prairie Grove was fought. During the battle the family took refuge in the cellar of their home. I mention incidentally that my father, Dr. Joel H. Blake, was surgeon in this battle and has told me that the women were a very great help to them in caring for the soldiers. After the battle, about sundown the women of this home went out on the battlefield among the wounded and dead. They carried in the wounded of both sides until their two rooms and porch were filled with men torn by shot and shell. All night they worked to relieve the sufferings of those who wore the blue as well as their own beloved grey. They tore up sheets and pillow slips for bandages, made hot, nourishing drinks of herbs, and gave freely of their scanty store. Two soldiers died that night, one in a blue uniform of the rank of captain. The other in a homespun suit of grey. The next morning those who were still living were taken to the old Presbyterian church and cared for until they were able to go away.

WOMEN DIGGING A GRAVE WITH A BROKEN HOE

This same Mrs. Staples together with a younger woman, with only boards and a broken hoe to dig with, dug a grave and buried a relative, a man too old and infirm to be in the army. The Federal scouts had burned his home and shot him. These brave girls worked till their hands were blistered and bleeding. They covered the grave with rocks and to this day one may pass the lonely mound, two miles east of Prairie Grove. Near by in a pasture is a broken elevation covered with grass, a large rock here and there and a lonely cedar tree. These bepeak a once happy home destroyed by the cruel hand of war. But now over all the place, the cattle browse, the birds sing, the flowers bloom, and all is peace.

------------ಅಸ್3·ಒ೪ಅ------------

A HUSBAND HANGED FOR HIS MONEY
By Mrs. O. M. Mashburn, of Saline County

I am now 78 years old. I was born in Georgia, but moved to Arkansas in 1856. My husband's home at the opening of the Civil war was in Saline County. Our little children and my brother, Tom Ball, made our home a happy one. My husband and brother soon joined the Confederate army and went through the war in safety.

COMING OF THE FEDERALS

When the Federals came to Little Rock scouting parties raided Saline County. The havoc and destruction cannot well be described. At that time we had plenty of stock, horses, cows, sheep and hogs. They took everything, even cutting the cloth from the looms, taking bed quilts and all clothing, except what the family was wearing at the time. Bread and water were our diet for many long stretches of time. They set fire to the house and cursed us for putting it out. It was a dreadful time.

HUSBAND HANGED BY FEDERALS

My husband came home on furlough just after the Federals had begun their raids. On one, occasion my husband was not watchful enough and they caught him. In some way they had heard that he had money hidden in the house. They hung him with his own bridle reins, leaving him half dead.

HORRORS OF THE BATTLEFIELD

The only battlefield that I ever visited was Hunter's Cross, on Hurricane creek. The wounded, dying and dead were all lying in heaps here and there. The moans of the wounded and the groans of the dying remained many long years in my memory.

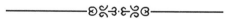

DIFFICULTIES OF LIFE OF CONFEDERATE WOMEN
By Mrs. W. D. Wasson, of Springtown

My father and brother joined the Confederate army and my mother was left with a large family of small children the oldest boy being only 13 years old. Father left us plenty to live on, but Federal soldiers came and destroyed everything. The hogs and cattle were killed, the corn taken and the fowls seized.

Federal soldiers were stationed at all the grist mills and no Southern woman was allowed entrance. Every country store outside of Fayetteville was burned to the ground and in Fayetteville a Southern woman could not buy or trade at the stores for either love or money (both of which they were short of).

MAKING SALT FROM SMOKE HOUSE CLAY

We dug up the dirt where the smoke houses were burned and put it in hoppers as is done in soap-making and the water was boiled down until there was a residue of salt. We burned an oval place in the tops of hard stumps and beat corn and wheat whenever they could be got. We bought by subscription a small handmill about the size of a sausage grinder and the neighboring women "came to mill" whenever they had anything. While one woman was grinding her corn, several would be on guard in trees and in outhouses watching for the Federals. We thought that the bread made from this meal was the best that we had ever eaten. We had splendid appetites; in fact, that was about all that we did have at times.

WOMEN BURIED TWO CONFEDERATES

Mrs. J. B. Stokes of Elm Springs, Ark., and Mrs. J. H. Wasson, now of Westville, I. T., went 20 miles in an ox cart and brought to their family burying ground the bodies of two Confederate soldiers that had been killed and partly burned. They dug the grave themselves, as there was no man on the place, and buried the dead as well as they could. The houses of these women had been burned to the ground and they were not allowed to take anything out of them. Two brave women, one a soldier's wife, the, other a young lady, walked 200 miles or more to Texas, carrying a small child and all their other worldly goods on their backs.

———————ତ୨୫ଃ୫ଓ———————

SOMEBODY'S DARLING
From Underwood's Women of the Confederacy.

Into a ward of the whitewashed halls
    Where the dead and dying lay;
Wounded by bayonets, shells and balls.
    Somebody's darling was borne one day.
Somebody's darling, so young and so brave,
    Wearing yet on his sweet, pale face,
Soon to be laid in the dust of the grave,
    The lingering light of his boyhood's grace.

Matted and damp are the curls of gold,
    Kissing the snow of that fair young brow;
Pale are the lips of delicate mould,

Somebody's darling is dying now.
Back from his beautiful blue-veined brow,
    Brush the wandering waves of gold;
Cross his hands on his bosom now —
    Somebody's darling is still and cold.

Kiss him once, for somebody's sake,
    Murmur a prayer, soft and low.
One bright curl from its fair mates take,
    They were somebody's pride, you know.
Somebody's hand hath rested there,
    Was it a mother's, soft and white;
Or have the lips of a sister fair
    Been baptized in their waves of light?

God knows best. He has somebody's love,
    Somebody's heart enshrined him there;
Somebody wafted his name above
    Night and morn, on the wings of prayer,
Somebody wept when he marched away,
    Looking so handsome, brave and grand.
Somebody's kiss on his forehead lay,
    Somebody clung to his parting hand.

Somebody's waiting, and watching for him,
    Yearning to hold him again to her heart,
And there he lies — with his blue eyes dim,
    And his smiling, child-like lips apart.
Tenderly bury the fair young dead,
    Pausing to drop o'er his grave a tear;
Carve on the wooden slab at his head,
    "Somebody's darling is lying here."

THE REBEL YELL

The old Rebel yell that used to nerve Johnnie Reb and frighten the life out of the Yanks, sounds something like the old steamboat whistle, one long, two short and one long cries. The yell was always begun at a low pitch, gradually rising to higher ones and getting lost in the heavens above if the charge was long continued. Another characteristic, and perhaps the one that contained the milk in the cocoanut, was that it should be a yelp, starting low and increasing with every bound as it bursted from several thousand throats of eager soldiers charging up hill or down hollow, made the very earth tremble and shook the courage out of Yankee hearts. Our Southern colleges should preserve this historic yell, which will be music to the ears of the old Rebs and their descendants.

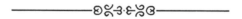

SHERMAN'S RAID
By *Miss Margaret E. Rush, of Union County*

My home is now in Union County, Ark. I was a small child in Anson County, N. C., during the war, where my mother, whose name was Elizabeth Myers, was born and raised. My father having died before the war, I had four sisters and one brother, who was forced to go to the war at the age of 17. He died six weeks later. If mother was living, she could tell better than I can of the hardships and troubles of that cruel war —

how hard it was to give up her only son and have to provide for a family of girls alone, and of the raid of Sherman's army, who destroyed the stock of provisions, house and furniture, and left the people to suffer the consequences with the few negroes.

I was small, but well do I remember seeing the Yankees riding the roads, with their horses loaded with meat, chickens, blankets and everything that they could carry. They burned the mills and gins. I saw Mr. Lockhart's gin burn. It was full of wheat and cotton. I can't tell half what we suffered from the effects of the war. I was raised without a man on the place, and had to do all kinds of work. I married a man here by the name of Rush. His father died in the war; his mother was left with her first-born to raise alone.

————————⊙❧⳾ℰℨ⳾❦⊙————————

ANDERSONVILLE VINDICATED
By Chas. Coffin, of Walnut Ridge

There is one thing concerning the conduct of the war that Northern people have held against us, and that is the treatment of Northern prisoners in Southern prisons. They have always held it as a blot on our record.

But we know the truth, and I think it is time they knew it. We know that the Northern soldiers in Southern prisons had the same rations in kind and quantity that guards over him had, and that the soldiers in the field had, with this difference: They were kept together in large numbers in a limited area, necessarily so, in a climate they were not assimilated to, and on a diet they were not accustomed to. Add to this then the fact that they were prisoners without hope, condemned to imprisonment during the war by their own government—for it was not the Confederate authorities who stopped the exchange of prisoners of war. The great military triumvirate of the North, Staunton, Grant, and Sherman were responsible for that. Everybody knows what Sherman said war was. Sherman said "War was hell!" and Staunton and Grant were wise enough to know that the Confederacy was playing with a limit—that they had only so many men out of whom it was possible to make soldiers, and if they could succeed in capturing and holding them it was only a question of time when the war must end; add to this the fact that the prisoners at Andersonville had among them an epidemic for which the doctors had no antidote, nostalgia—homesickness—the direst of all diseases, for it has its origin in that "hope deferred" that makes the heart sick even unto death. Under these conditions, of course they sickened and died.

But I submit if in the good year of our Lord, 1898, at a time when our doctors have become intimately familiar with bacilli and bacteria, the germs of disease and death; when the science of surgery has reached a higher degree of skill and excellence than was ever before known; if under these conditions the United States, with all the resources, financial and material at her command, has been unable to keep disease and death away from Chickamauga, how in Heavens name I ask you, could the impoverished Confederacy have been expected to keep them away from Andersonville in 1864! In the light of the history of Chickamauga in 1898, Andersonville in 1864, stands absolutely vindicated.

A NORTHERN WAR NURSE

The most famous Sister of Charity who went out with the Northern Army was probably Sister Anthony of Cincinnati, who accompanied the hospital corps of the army of General Rosecrantz. She was a fine business woman, a tender nurse, and the possessor of that mysterious power which is called personal magnetism. After the close of the war, so great and general was her reputation, that two gentlemen of Cincinnati, not of her faith, presented her with the magnificent Samaritan Hospital of that city, as a mark of their high appreciation of her character. The only draw-back she ever felt was from her looks. She was as homely as the Lord ever made a woman. On one occasion when caring for the sick and wounded in the hospital, she went to a meat market in Cincinnati, to buy a few chickens. She complained about the high price. The dealer made some rough remark, to which she paid no attention. Then he used more rough language, and as she persisted, money being scarce, he said finally, "Oh take them along for anything. You are so d—d ugly I cannot talk to you any more. If you were good looking I would talk an hour."

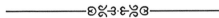

SOUTHERN CROSS OF HONOR
From the Official Circular of U. D. C.

The idea of the Southern Cross of Honor to be given by the United Daughters of the Confederacy to the veterans and descendants of deceased Confederate soldiers and sailors originated with Mrs. Mary Ann Cobb Erwin, Athens, Ga.

The design offered by Mrs. S. E. Gabbett, Atlanta, Ga., Chairman of the committee appointed by Mrs. Katie Cabell Currie, President U. D. C., at Hot Springs, Ark., November, 1898, to procure designs, was accepted at Richmond, Va., November, 1899. The members of the committee were Mrs. S. E. Gabbett, Chairman, Atlanta, Ga.; Mrs. C. Helen Plane, Atlanta, Ga.; Mrs. Mary Ann Cobb Erwin, Athens, Ga. Upon the resignation of Mrs. Erwin, Miss Mildred Lewis Rutherford, Athens, Ga., was appointed in her place.

The rules formulated by this committee were found insufficient to meet the many questions that arose regarding the bestowal of the Cross, so at the request of Mrs. Gabbett, who had been appointed Custodian of the Cross at Richmond, 1899, Mrs. Edwin G. Weed, President of U. D. C., enlarged the committee at Montgomery, Ala., November, 1900.

The members of this committee are Mrs. Cornelia Branch Stone, Galveston, Texas, Chairman; Mrs. Virginia Faulkner McSherry, West Va.; Mrs. J. W. Lench, Florida; Mrs. J. W Thompson, Florida; Mrs. Beede, California; Mrs. Poe, Maryland; Mrs. L. H. Raines, of Georgia.

RULES FOR BESTOWAL OF CROSS OF HONOR

RULE I

SECTION 1. Each State and Territorial Division shall elect, or appoint a Recorder of Cross of Honor, to whom Chapters shall apply for blank certificates of eligibility, to be filled out by the veterans, and blank forms for alphabetical lists, to be filled out with data from the certificates, by the President of the Chapter ordering crosses. When so filled out these shall be sent to the Recorder of said Division, for approval, or correction, and forwarded by her to the Custodian of the Cross, who will forward the Crosses to the Chapter.

The Recorder shall apply to the Recording Secretary General, U. D. C., for the blank forms of certificates, and blank forms of alphabetical lists, supplying these, on demand, to the Chapters, accompanied by an order to the Custodian, signed by the President General and Recording Secretary General, U. D. C.

SEC. 2. The oldest living lineal descendants of Veterans, who have not received a Cross, may secure it in any county, provided, that three consecutive monthly notices be inserted in the city and county papers, calling upon Veterans to send in certificates for crosses. If at the expiration of three months, there are no other applications from veterans, the bestowal of Crosses upon such descendants, may begin; the same to be governed by rules for bestowal upon Veterans. Where there is no lineal descendant desiring the Cross, it may be bestowed upon the widow of a veteran, who has not received a Cross, provided she be a Confederate woman, who has endured the hardships and privations of the period from "sixty-one to sixty-five." No descendant or widow can receive a second Cross, nor can such descendant or widow wear the cross. The Recording Secretary General will supply to the Recorder of Cross of Honor of each State and Territorial Division special blank forms of certificates, for descendants and widows, which must be filled out with data of eligibility of ancestor or husband.

RULE II

SECTION 1. No Crosses will be furnished by the Custodian unless the order is accompanied by certificates of eligibility, properly filled out, by the Veterans, and certified to, by two, or more, members of a Camp of United Confederate Veterans, and alphabetical list, from Chapter President.

SEC. 2. Presidents of Chapters shall fill out blank alphabetical lists from the certificates with all data contained therein to forward with certificates to their State Recorder of Cross of Honor, with money order, for the number of Crosses desired.

The Custodian of the Cross of Honor shall keep a book, or books, in which, shall be kept, alphabetically arranged, the names and data of all Veterans, descendants of Veterans, and widows to whom Crosses have been issued.

SEC. 3. The certificates shall be returned by the Custodian to the Presidents of Chapters who have ordered Crosses and the same be placed on file, by said Chapter, that data may be furnished when needed for historical, or other purpose.

SEC. 4. Each Chapter shall keep a book, alphabetically arranged, in which is recorded the name and service of every Veteran, and ancestor or descendant, and widow, of a veteran, who receives a Cross. Each State or Territorial Recorder shall keep a similar record book of all Crosses issued.

RULE III

SECTION 1. Crosses may be granted by the muster roll of the nearest Camp, U. C. V., and to Confederate Veterans who are not members of a Camp, who can give the required proof of eligibility, attested by two Veterans who are members of a Camp.

SEC. 2. The oldest living lineal descendant may secure the Cross, by giving the same proof of eligibility as that required of his Veteran ancestor—and Confederate widows of Veterans applying for Cross, must fill blank form of certificate, giving service of Veteran, whose widow she is—such widows must have endured the hardships of the war period from 1861 to 1865.

SEC. 3. Upon the certificate of a reputable physician that a Veteran is dying, if desired, he may receive the Cross immediately.

RULE IV

SECTION 1. The Crosses may be bestowed on the Memorial or Decoration Day, selected by each State or Territorial Division, U. D. C.; the birthdays of President Jefferson Davis and General Robert E. Lee—June 3rd and January 19th; and one commemorative day, between July 1st and January 19th, to be selected by each State or Territorial Division, in convention assembled. The presentation shall be accompanied with such ceremonies as will give proper dignity to the occasion.

RULE V

SECTION 1. A Veteran, in good standing, having lost his Cross, may have it replaced once, only, by applying to the President of the Chapter from which he received the Cross, and he must furnish copy of the certificate on which the Cross was first bestowed. If a second Cross is lost, a certificate may be given, in testimony that such Veteran has been awarded a Cross. No descendant, or widow, of a Veteran, can have a second Cross.

SEC. 2. Chapter Presidents are urged to advise Veterans to have their names engraved on the bar of Cross, for the purpose of identification, if lost.

SEC. 3. A Veteran having been awarded a Cross, and dying before it is received, the President of the Chapter bestowing it may give it to the oldest living, lineal descendant, or widow, under provisions of Rule I, Sec. 2. A Veteran having received the Cross, may bequeath it to any lineal descendant that he may select.

RULE VI

The Cross cannot be worn, in any case, or on any occasion, except by the Veteran upon whom it was bestowed—no descendant or widow can wear it.

RULE VII

SECTION 1. Where counties have no local organization of U. D. C., a Veteran may receive the Cross through the President of the nearest local Chapter, or the President of Chapter in the county from which he entered the Confederate Service, if so desired.

SEC. 2. When Chapters are not able to bear the expense of purchasing Crosses for other counties than their own, these may he furnished at the expense of the General Association, upon the authority of the President General, U. D. C.

RULE VIII

All orders for Crosses shall be filed in the Custodian's office three weeks before the day intended for bestowal.

RULE IX.

Any Chapter departing from these rules will not be entitled to Crosses for presentation.

Preceding the presentation of the Crosses, Rules V, VI, VII, VIII, and IX, shall be read, on every occasion of the bestowal.

The President of each Chapter shall see that the Camps of Confederate Veterans and Sons of Confederate Veterans in her county shall receive a copy of these rules for continual reference.

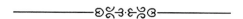

HISTORY OF CONFEDERATE UNIFORM AND FLAG

Designs From Which They Were Adopted Were Made by Nicola Marschall, a Prussian Artist, Who for More than Thirty Years Has Lived in Louisville—He Prepared the Drawings at the Request of Mrs. Napoleon Lockett in Marion, Ala., Where He Resided Then.

Located in Louisville, in a well-known business building, is a time-stained yet time-honored room. Its walls are darkened with the finger marks of the passing years, and, the whole demeanor of the place is unobtrusive and unpretentious. Yet is this place rich in its treasured traditions of the Old South or the southland of ante-bellum days.

It is the art studio of Nicola Marschall, musician, portrait painter and designer of both uniform and flag of the Confederate States of America. From his Prussian homeland, where he was made skilfull musically and trained to the painter's art, this man, then in his youth, came over land and sea to America at one of the most rugged and picturesque periods of this country's history, the memorable gold-fever days of '49. It was in Alabama that he found the home for which he sought. With no other compensation than the pride it caused him to serve the South, and the pleasure it gave him to honor a woman's request, these designs were made by Nicola Marschall in 1861, and adopted by the Southern Confederacy.

Mr. Marschall's studio is in the building on the southwest corner of Green and Fourth streets. It is a veritable curiosity shop, a place wealthy in historic recollections, its souvenirs of bygone days and the works of this artist. There are many portraits about the place, portraits that show upon canvas the mental pictures still dear to the people of the South. Portraits of Robt. E. Lee, Joseph E. Johnston, J. C. Breckenridge, William Preston and Genl. Bragg are among those in his studio These are but a few of the Confederate leaders whose portraits he has painted. Among the best pictures he has ever painted were two of Gen. N. B. Forrest, the "Wizard of the Saddle," who was the personal friend of Mr. Marschall.

There is probably no souvenir, among those Mr. Marschall has more interesting than a letter introducing him to President Jefferson Davis, written by Gen. N. B. Forrest. The letter was written in 1872 when General Forrest was president of the old Selma, Marion & Memphis Railroad. General Forrest lived in Marion, Ala., then, at which place Mr. Marschall made his home, and it was when the latter contemplated going to Memphis where President Davis was then, that the letter was written. It was reproduced in facsimile made from the original, secured for the purpose through the courtesy of Mr. Marschall.

The story of how Mr. Marschall came to design the uniform and flag of the Confederacy is best told in his own words.

"I came to this country," he began, "when I was eighteen years of age. My home was in St. Wendel, Prussia, and I left there that I might continue professionally with music and art, instead of having to serve in the army. I left with the permission of my Government, something more easily obtained then than now. I landed in New Orleans and from there made my way to Mobile, where lived a relative of mine, who had preceded me here. I met him on the eve of his departure for California. It was in 1849 that I landed in America, when the tide of humanity was flowing toward the gold fields of the Pacific coast.

"My kinsman tried to persuade me to join his mining party and go to California in search of wealth. But I was then as far away from home as I cared to be, and so declined to go. I became acquainted with one of the teachers in the female seminary at Marion, Ala., and learned that it was one of the garden spots of the South. Wealthy planters lived there; it was a seat of learning and claimed as citizens many of the oldest and most aristocratic Southern families. I decided to go to Marion, and go I did. I became a teacher at the seminary there, where I taught painting, violin, piano, guitar and the French and German languages.

"My studies in Europe of drawing and painting now served me well. I came over here on an old sailing vessel, and well do I remember to this day how I had to draw the picture of every member of the crew from captain to humblest sailor. I had been in this country one year when my brother arrived here from Prussia.

"In 1857 I returned to Prussia and remained in Prussia for two years continuing my studies of art. I studied both in Munich and Italy. It was while returning from Italy and passing through Verona, which then belonged to Austria, that I saw the uniform which some years later was to furnish me the design for the Southern Confederate uniform.

"In Verona one day the notes of martial music came to me. On searching out I found that a party of sharpshooters belonging to the Austrian army were passing.

" 'What splendid soldiers and what noble uniforms,' was my involuntary comment as I saw them. Well might this be said. They were all great manly soldiers and were dressed in the striking uniform of gray with green trimmings. The green denoted their branch of the army—the sharpshooters—and their rank was indicated by marks on the collars of their coats, bars for Lieutenants and Captains, stars for the higher officers.

"I returned to America in 1859 and again located in Marion. There I painted many portraits of the wealthy planters and members of their families, as well as of other prominent people of the South. Andrew Moore was then a judge at Marion. He afterwards became War Governor of Alabama, and was one of the most important men in those days in our part of the country.

"Mrs. Napoleon Lockett, a beautiful Southern woman of an old Virginia family and the wife of a wealthy planter, lived at Marion. Her eldest son married the eldest daughter of Governor Moore and one of her younger sons married one of the younger daughters of Governor Moore.

"Soon came the first notes of war. Mrs. Lockett was as loyal a daughter as the South had, and was much interested in its affairs then. She came to me one day and said: 'Mr. Marschall, we have seceded, and the Confederate Government wants a flag. Will you make us a design? It must not be too unlike the United States flag, but different enough to be distinguished at a distance.'

"At once I took pencil and paper, and made three different designs. The first was of two red stripes and one of white, with a blue field bearing seven white stars—indicating the number of states that had then seceeded—in the upper left-hand corner. The second design was the same, except that the blue field with stars was at the extreme left of the white stripe, instead of the top red stripe. The third design had the two full red stripes at top and bottom, the white stripe in the middle with the blue field and white stars in the center."

It is a matter of historical fact that this first design, made by Mr. Marschall was the flag adopted by the Confederate Government. It is also well known to those familiar with Southern history that this flag—the Stars and Bars—was placed on the staff above the capitol at Montgomery, Alabama, on March 4, 1861, by Miss J. C. Tyler, of Virginia. She was a granddaughter of John Tyler, ex-President of the United States.

Continuing his interesting narrative, Mr. Marschall said: "Mrs. Lockett thanked me for the flag designs. Then she came back, adding: 'We also want a design for a uniform, Mr. Marschall. Can't you suggest one?' The thought occurred to me of the gray uniforms I had seen worn by the Austrian sharpshooters. I took a piece of paper and made several rough sketches, indicating the gray color, and also the colors on the collars to denote the branch of the service—buff for officers, yellow for cavalry, blue for infantry red for artillery, etc. "It did not occur to me then that I had done anything worthy of note. I simply made the sketches at the request of Mrs. Lockett. I knew no more about them from then, until I found that the uniform and one of the flags had been adopted by the Confederacy."

This is the story of how the gray of the Confederate army and the banner under which that army fought, were made—a story told by the one who conceived the plans. Not boastfully but with a measure of pride does Mr. Marschall, when sought out, tell the story. He considers that he had done little in making the designs, but he is to this day proud that his were the ideas adopted for both the uniform and the flag of the South.

When war was declared Mr. Marschall enlisted as a private of volunteers going with his command from Marion to garrison Forts Morgan and Gaines at the mouth of Mobile Bay. There he served for a time then returned to Marion on a furlough. While at home, on the advice of a friend, an officer, he employed a substitute for a year and three months. Then came the call for more volunteers, and again Mr. Marschall enlisted, this time in the second Alabama regiment of engineers. He served with Colonel Lockett, a son of Mrs. Napoleon Lockett under General Polk, just preceding the fall of Vicksburg. Mr. Marschall served then in the Confederate army until the curtain was finally drawn at Appomattox.

Mr. Marschall numbered among his close friends Maj. Jabez Currie, one of Alabama's wealthiest planters, and an uncle of Dr. J. L. M. Currie. It was at the suggestion of Major Currie, who had friends in Kentucky, that Mr. Marschall came to Louisville to live. He returned to his art after the war, and many are the treasured portraits in halls and homes of the South today that stand as the product of his brush. Louisville became the home of his adoption in 1873. On arriving here he located in the studio he occupies today, never in all that time having made a change.

Marion, Ala., Nov. 11, 1872.

Mr. Jefferson Davis, Memphis, Tenn.,

Dear Sir:-This letter will introduce to you my friend, Mr. Nicola Marschall, of this city, who visits Memphis for the purpose of examining our city with a view of locating. He is a true Southerner, was with us in our troubles, and is one of the finest artists we have. I hope he may be pleased with our city. Any favors shown him will be duly appreciated by him and thankfully received by your friend, etc.,

N. B. FORREST.

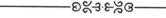

FLAGS OF THE CONFEDERACY
OFFICIALLY DESCRIBED

Owing to incorrect representations in historical works, incorrect reproductions and representations by manufactures of flags and badges, and in pictorial publications of all kinds; to frequent inquiries in the press and the erroneous answers thereto, and to general lack of exact information regarding the flags of the Confederate States of America, the United Confederate Veterans some years ago deemed it necessary to appoint a committee empowered to make a diligent investigation and report their finding to that body, says the New York Herald. In June, 1894, this committee made a report of its labors, and the United Confederate Veterans, that were then assembled at Nashville, passed a resolution as follows:

"That in order to give the impress of authority for the guidance of all persons it is hereby declared to be the conclusive judgment of this organization that the flags of the Confederate States of America were established by legislation of the Congress of the Confederate States and otherwise in the manner fully set forth in the accompanying report of the committee on flags of this organization, and that said report is hereby adopted."

A pamphlet very attractively prepared and with the pictures of the flags in colors has recently been issued. The title page contains the battle flag and bears these words: "The flags of the Confederate States of America—by authority of the United Confederate Veterans."

The flag committee was composed of Samuel E. Lewis, M. D., of Washington, D. C., chairman; Fred L. Robertson of Tallahassee, Fla.; J. F. Shipp, Chattanooga, Term.; J. Taylor Ellyson, Richmond, Va., and A. C. Trippe of Baltimore, Md. The committee's full report as approved in 1904, Stephen D. Lee, general commanding, and William E. Mickle, adjutant-general and chief of staff, is given in abridged form in the pamphlet, and describes the various flags as follows:

OFFICIAL DESCRIPTION OF FLAGS

"The Stars and Bars—The flag recommended by the 'committee on a proper flag for the Confederate States of America,' appointed by the Provisional Congress, in its report of March 4, 1861, is as follows: 'That the flag of the Confederate States of America shall consist of a red field, with a white space extending horizontally through the center and equal in width to one-third the width of the flag; the red spaces above and below to be of the same width as the white; the union blue extending down through the white space and stopping at the lower red space. In the center of the union a circle of white stars, corresponding in number with the states in

the Confederacy.' The union is square; the stars five-
pointed; the length of the flag is one and a half times the
width.

"The Battle Flag—The battle flag is square, having a
Greek cross (salter) of blue, edged with white, with
thirteen equal white five-pointed stars, upon a red field,
the whole bordered with white. There are three sizes:
Infantry, 48 inches square; artillery, 36 inches square;
cavalry, 30 inches square. The proportions for an infantry flag are: 48 inches by 48 inches (exclusive of the
border); the blue arms of the cross, 1 1-2 inches wide;
the white edging to the cross, 1-2 inch wide; the white
border around the flag proper, 1 1-2 inches wide. Total
outside measurement, 51 inches. The stars are five-
pointed, inscribed within a circle of 6 inches diameter,
and are of uniform size. There should be five eyelet
holes in the hoist, next the pole. The artillery and cavalry flags are correspondingly reduced in all proportions.

"The National Flag, established May 1, 1863, is as
follows: 'The Congress of the Confederate States of
America do enact, That the flag of the Confederate
States shall be as follows: The field to be white, the
length double the width of the flag, with the union (now
used as the battle flag) to be a square of two-thirds the
width of the flag, having the ground red; thereon a
broad salter of blue, bordered with white, and emblazoned with white mullets or five-pointed stars, corresponding in number to that of the Confederate States.'

"The National Flag, established March 4, 1865, is as
follows: 'The Congress of the Confederate States of
America do enact, That the flag of the Confederate
States shall be as follows: The width two-thirds of its

length, with the union (now used as the battle flag) to be in width three-fifths of the width of the flag, and so proportioned as to leave the length of the field on the side of the union twice the width of the field below it; to have the ground red and a broad, blue salter thereon, bordered with white and emblazoned with mullets or five-pointed stars, corresponding in number to that of the Confederate States; the field to be white, except the outer half from the union to be a red bar extending the width of the flag.'

FLOWN BY CONFEDERATE NAVY

"The Stars and Bars (previously described)—The new ensign, pennant, and jack, by order of the secretary of the navy, May 26, 1863, is as follows: 'The new ensign will be made according to the following directions, viz.: The field to be white, the length one and a half times the width of the flag, with the union (now used as the battle flag) to be square, of two-thirds of the width of the flag, having the ground red, thereon a broad salter of blue, to the union as 1, 4 4-5, bordered with white, to the union as 1.22, and emblazoned with white mullets. or five-pointed stars diameter of stars to union as 1.6 2-5, corresponding in number to that of the Confederate States.'

"The Pennant—A white ground, its size to be as 1.72, or its length seventy-two times its width at the head, and tapering to a point. The union of the pennant to be as follows: All red from the head for three times its width, with white border equal to twelve times its width, to be emblazoned with stars, in number equal to those in the ensign, with a white border equal to half the width, and then red three times the width, with the fly all white.

"The Jack—To be the same as the union for the ensign, except that its length shall be one and a half times it width."

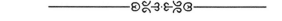

THE WOMEN OF THE CONFEDERACY, GOD BLESS THEM
By General C. Irvine Walker

How glorious were the achievements of our Confederate women and how gladly we should unite in erecting to their memory the beautiful series of monuments the committee has planned. First, we will select the grandest, most inspiring design that is offered, and then throughout the Southland, we will raise on high in each State, this beautiful emblem of the devotion and patriotism of our Confederate women, attesting for all time to come the love and admiration of those who "knew them but to love them." These monuments will teach patriotism and devotion to generations yet unborn, and will create in the hearts of all who see them a desire to emulate the splendid virtues of those in whose honor they were created. As Judge Anthony M. Keiley once eloquently said: "It was not the history of the heroes, but their statues in the Ceramicus that would not allow the young son of Philip to sleep."

Veterans, how strongly this movement must appeal to you! When in 1861, the South rose in her might and declared that she would defend, by force of arms, the liberties that belonged to her people, the Southern woman brushed away her tears, and sent you forth to battle for the right; when wounded and torn she bore you from the bloody field; it was her hand that soothed the burning pains, and her voice that cheered you back to health again, and when home she brought her first-born son, a hero martyred upon the altar of the father-land, she stifled her sobs in her bosom, and with her blessing a younger son left for the front to close the widening breach in that fatal firing line. When at last, crushed by overwhelming numbers and worn out by long years of fierce fighting against tremendous odds, you laid down the arms with which you had wrought for yourselves crowns of undying fame, "When the stars upon your banner had gone back to the heavens from which they came;" when you returned broken-hearted at your cause's fall, to find your homes laid desolate by the ruthless hand of long continued war; when you were called upon to face the horrors of those dark days of the reconstruction, she was by your side, and by precept and by example, she taught you to be as noble in defeat as you had been grand in battle. Reared in the lap of luxury, accustomed to every comfort that wealth could bring, she accepted poverty for your sake without a murmur. Hiding in the sacred recesses of her heart the grief she felt for dear ones lost and a cause forever dead, she set herself to the task of bringing back the smile to your face and happiness to your heart, until inspired by her example, you have brushed away all ob-stacles, and have made this fair Southland of ours to bloom and blossom like the rose.

Sons of Confederate veterans, how plain your duty is! You are the sons of those noble women, and you are the sons of the men, engaged in a righteous cause, whose hands they sought to uphold. You have as a precious heritage the proud knowledge that your father was a Confederate soldier, and that your mother was a Confederate woman, and you and your children and children's children should rise up and call their memory blessed. It has been said of the United Sons of Confederate veterans that they are "banded together for the purpose of soothing the declining years of those who bore, unflinchingly, the burden of that tremendous struggle, and of handing down to future generations the true story of a great lost cause." How better can we tell the story than in imperishable marble and bronze? The Southland is dotted with monuments Southern women have erected to Confederate valor; every cemetery where the heroes sleep is beautiful by their tender care; every page of our history is made sacred by the devotion with which they consecrated their loyalty, but hardly a single visible mark stands today to give evidence of the appreciation of their countrymen. Now, it is proposed to declare to the people of the world the South's unbounded admiration for our Confederate mothers.

Without the fierce passions of the conflict to sustain her, with no hope of fame or glory as the reward of great deeds nobly done; but prompted only by patriotism and a deep devotion to her country's cause, she suffered in silence more than tongue can tell, and accomplished as much as to entitle her to be held as the dearest of all our memories. Let's build these monuments grand, inspiring and beautiful; let's have every line of them breathe tenderness and devotion; let's erect them out among the trees amid the grass and the flowers in our most beautiful public places. Let every

Southern heart be glad because we are about to do this honor to the Southern women of war times; let the hand of every Southerner reach forth generously to make his willing contribution to this fund.

———————ഇ⅗⅗⅗ഇ———————

CONFEDERATE GENERALS, LIEUTENANT-GENERALS, AND MAJOR-GENERALS
By Rev. I. William Jones.

The death of General Longstreet and of General Gordon has caused some confused statements about the generals and lieutenant-generals of the Confederacy, and it may be well to give the full list in the order of their rank.

The full generals were:

1. Samuel Cooper.
2. Albert Sydney Johnston.
3. Robert Edward Lee.
4. Joseph E. Johnston.
5. Gustave T. Beauregard.
6. Braxton Bragg.
General Provisional Army, E. Kirby Smith.
General with temporary rank, J. B. Hood.

LIEUTENANT-GENERALS

1. James Longstreet.
2. E. Kirby Smith.
3. Leonidas Polk.

4. Theophilus H. Holmes.
5. William J. Hardee.
6. Thomas J. Jackson.
7. John C. Pemberton.
8. Richard S. Ewell.
9. Ambrose Power Hill.
10. Daniel H. Hill.
11. John B. Hood.
12. Richard Taylor.
13. Stephen D. Lee.
14. Jubal A. Early.
15. Richard H. Anderson.
16. Alexander P. Stewart.
17. Nathan Bedford Forrest.
18. Wade Hampton.
19. Simon B. Buckner.
20. Joseph Wheeler.

General John B. Gordon was appointed lieutenant-general by President Davis just after his brilliant capture of Fort Stedman, but his commission did not reach him before the evacuation, and although he commanded a corps for some time, and on the retreat was put by General Lee in command of one wing of the army, he always wrote "major-general" as his real rank. The same practically was true of General Fitzhugh Lee, who commanded the cavalry corps after General Hampton was sent South.

The "full generals" have all long since crossed the river, and of the lieutenant-generals, only General S. D. Lee, General S. B. Buckner and General A. P. Stewart remain.

And, alas! the major-generals, the brigadiers, the other officers of the "field and staff," and the rank and file of the Confederate armies are stepping out of ranks so rapidly that soon there will be none left to answer the roll call down here.

In addition to the above, seventy-seven Confederate soldiers attained the rank of major-general whose names alphabetically arranged are:

Henry W. Allen, William W. Allen, Jr., Patton Anderson, William B. Bate, John S. Bowen, John C. Breckinridge, John C. Brown, Matthew C. Butler, Benjamin F. Cheatham, Henry D. Clayton, Thomas J. Churchill, Pat R. Cleburne, George B. Crittenden, Daniel S. Donelson, Arnold Elzey, James F. Fagan, Charles W. Field, John B. Floyd, John H. Forney, Samuel G. French, Martin W. Gary, Jeremy F. Gilmer, M. W. Gray, Bryan Grimes, Harry T. Hays, Henry Heth, Thomas C. Hindman, Robert F. Hoke, Benjamin Huger, William Y. C. Humes, Bushrod R. Johnson, Edward Johnson, David R. Jones, Samuel Jones, James L. Kemper, Joseph B. Kershaw, Evander M. Law, Fitzhugh Lee, George W. C. Lee, William H. F. Lee, Lunsford L. Lomax, William W. Loring, Mansfield Lovell, John T. Magruder, William Mahone, John S. Marmaduke, William T. Martin, Dabney H. Maury, Samuel B. Maxey, John P. McCown, Lafayette McLaws, Mosby M. Parsons, John Pegram, William D. Pender, William M. Pendleton, George M. Pickett, Camille J. Polignac. Thomas L. Rosser, Gustavus W. Smith, Martin L. Smith, William Smith, Carter L. Stevenson, J. E. B. Stewart, William B. Taliaferro, Isaac R. Trimble, David E. Twiggs, Earl Van Dorn,

John G. Walker, William T. Walker, William H. C. Whiting, Cadmus M. Wilcox and Ambrose R. Wright.

THE BISHOPS IN THE WAR

Well do we remember the departure of Bishop Polk from Richmond to seek the advice of Bishop Meade, then the senior of the House of Bishops, at his home in Northern Virginia.

"And what did he tell you?" we said.

"I saluted him," said the good bishop, "and said to him: 'Sir, I have been offered a commission in the Confederate army, and have come to ask your advice.' His reply was:

"Sir, you hold already a higher commission than that in the church militant."

"I am aware of that, right reverend sir; and I do not intend to resign it, but hope to hold it in the church triumphant."

"Well, the senior bishop did not give his consent then?"

"Yes, he did," said Bishop Polk, with a twinkle in his eye and a confident manner that was peculiarly his own. "Yes, he did; I quoted scripture to him, and we talked the matter all over thoroughly, and he finally told me if I felt it my duty to accept, I had his full consent, and so say all the rest of my brethren."

Most of these bishops were not chaplains, but fighting men. Being soldiers of the cross seemed to have stimulated them for the real fray. Bishop T. U. Dudley of Kentucky and Bishop R. W. B. Elliott of Texas were immediately associated in the service, and the latter was severely wounded. Bishop George W. Petererkin of West Virginia was paroled at Appomattox, having been first Lieutenant and aide to Gen. W. N. Pendleton of Lexington, Virginia, an eminent Episcopal divine.

Bishop Samuel S. Harris of Michigan was a gallant soldier from Alabama, and Leonidas Polk of Louisiana, mentioned above, was a lieutenant general when killed at Pine Mount near Marietta, Georgia. Reverend Dr. Martin Parks of North Carolina resigned from the old army in 1828 to become a clergyman. He was elected to a bishopric in Alabama, but declined.

Our own two beloved bishops in Florida were "soldiers of war." Rt. Rev. Edwin C. Weed having been a cavalry soldier in a Georgia regiment, and Rt. Rev. William Crane Grey having served as chaplain in a Tennessee regiment. And thus

"The sons of God go forth to war,
A kingly crown to gain."

Note—To the above may be added Bishop Ellison Capers of South Carolina, who was a brigadier general in the Confederate army.

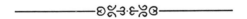

LETTER FROM CONFEDERATE WOMEN
TO THE SOLDIERS

The following is an open letter from Confederate women to the soldiers in the field, published during the war:

"Soldiers:—The president, congress, the public press and your generals have told you the high esteem of your noble devotion in re-enlisting for the war. We also, as your mothers, wives, daughters, sisters and friends, claim the right to thank you. It is the grandest act of the revolution and secures immortality to all concerned in it. It awakens anew the enthusiasm with which we began this struggle for liberty, and removes all doubt of its eventual success. Such men in such a cause cannot be overcome. In the dreariness of camp life you may have sometimes imagined yourselves forgotten or little cared for. Counting up your privations and dangers you may have doubted their full appreciation, and fancied that those who stay at home and risk nothing, while you suffer and bleed, are more esteemed than yourselves.

"We beseech you harbor no such thought. You are constantly present to our minds. The women of the South bestow all the respect and affection upon the heroes who defend them against a barbarous and cruel foe. In the resolution to aid you, they are as firm and determined as you in yours, not to lay down your arms until independence be won. When that sacred vow shall have been accomplished your reception by us will more than attest our sincerity. It shall be shown while the contest goes on, by our efforts to increase your comforts in the field and to lighten the burdens of the dear ones left at home. For your stricken country's sake and ours be true to yourselves and our glorious cause. Never turn your back on the flag, nor desert the ranks of honor or the post of danger. Men guilty of such infamy sell your blood and our honor, and give up the Confederacy to its wicked invaders. In after years from generation to generation the black title of tory and deserter will cling to them, disgracing their children's children. But no stigma like this will stain you and yours. Brave, patriotic and self-sacrificing in time of war, you will be honored in peace as the saviours of your country, and the pride and glory of your Countrywomen. We beg to keep near your hearts our memorials of affection and respect, and to remember them especially in battle, and we invoke for you always the protection of a kind and merciful Providence."

ORIGINAL VERSION OF DIXIE

Following are the original words of Dixie:

> I wish I was in de land ob cotton,
> Cinnamon seed and sandy bottom;
>   Look, away, look away, away.
> Dixie land.
> In Dixie land where I was born in
> Early on one frosty mornin,'
>   Look away, look away, away.

CHORUS

Den I wish I was in Dixie,
    Hooray! Hooray!
In Dixie land I'll take my stand,
    To lib an' die in Dixie,
Away, away, away down south in Dixie.

Old Missus marry Will de Weaber,
William was a gay deceiber;
When he put his arms around 'er,
He looked as fierce as a forty-pounder

Chorus: Hooray! Hooray! etc.

His face was sharp like a butcher's cleaber,
But dat did not seem to greab 'er;
Will run away, Missus took a de cline, O!
Her face was de color ob bacon shine, O!

Chorus: Hooray! Hooray! etc.

While Missus libbed, she libbed in Clober;
When she died, she died all ober,
How could she act such foolish part, O!
An' marry a man to break her heart, O!

Chorus: Hooray! Hooray! etc.

Buckwheat cakes an' stony batter,
Makes you fat or a little fatter;
Here's a health to de next old Missus.
And all de gals dat want to kiss us.

Chorus: Hooray! Hooray! etc.

Now if you want to drive away sorrow,
Come an' hear dis song tomorrow,
Den hot it down an' scratch de grabble,
To Dixie's land I'm bound to trabble.

Chorus: Hooray! Hooray! etc.

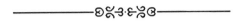

GENERAL GRANT SWORN TO SECRECY
BY A LITTLE GIRL

An interesting story in which a little girl and General Grant played the conspicuous parts was told by one of the Confederate veterans that was at the reunion in Nashville during the centennial year.

He was one of the younger soldiers that went out to fight for his country. Being dangerously wounded, he was taken home on parole. Soon after his return, General Grant appeared upon the scene and took up headquarters in the old southern mansion.

The family becoming alarmed for the safety of the boy, he was with much difficulty hidden under the house, the intervening space between the ground and the floor being very narrow. Even then their fears were not lessened, for to their anxious ears every groan beneath was fearfully audible. So an elder sister, to relieve the situation, sat at the piano and played and sang all through the day. The intense strain of the passing hours growing monotonous to the child of the household, she decided to take affairs into her own hands without any consultation.

As General Grant sat in his room late in the afternoon there came a soft tap at his door. In answer to his invitation to enter there appeared a demure little maiden with a mass of tangled curls and cheeks of the reddest hue. She walked gravely up before him, and looking him in the face, said:

"I've got something to tell you."

"You have? I shall be very glad to hear it."

"Well, before I tell you, you've got to promise that you'll never, never tell. Do you declare and cross your heart and wish you may die in a minute if you ever, ever tell?"

The general preserved his dignity and answered, "Yes."

"Well, then do it." and he repeated the words after her and made the movement as she directed. Then there came a whisper:

"My big brother is sick under the house; he's out there with the bugs and rats, and they're going to eat him up."

As a result of the disclosure the master of the house, meeting the general in the hallway somewhat later, was startled by this speech being addressed to him:

The dignified figure of the father assumed even greater dignity.

"I hear you have a wounded son under the house.

"What is that to you?"

"Simply this: if he is in need of medical attention, he should have it and be placed in comfortable quarters for receiving it."

Had the little girl's voice not been raised for the big brother, it is uncertain whether he would ever have been able to greet his comrades at a reunion, but the part she played in the drama was never known until years later, when she summoned courage to tell the family.

Whether the general ever betrayed his trust has not been revealed.

ARMY ORDER OF GENERAL LEE
AT CHAMBERSBURG, PA.

The following was issued by General Lee at Chambersburg, Pa.:

Headquarters. Army of Northern Virginia, Chambersburg, Pa., 27th June, 1863. General Orders No. 73.

The Commanding General has observed with marked satisfaction the conduct of the troops on the march and confidently anticipates results commensurate with the high spirit they have manifested.

No troops could have displayed better fortitude, or better performed the arduous marches of the past ten days.

Their conduct in other respects has, with few exceptions, been in keeping with their character as soldiers and entitles them to approbation and praise. There have, however, been instances of forgetfulness on the part of some, that they have in keeping the yet unsullied reputation of this army, and that the duties exacted of us by civilization and Christianity are not less obligatory in the country of the enemy than in our own.

The Commanding General considers that no greater disgrace could befall the army, and through it our whole people than the perpetration of the barbarous outrages upon the unarmed and defenceless, and the wanton destruction of private property, that have marked the course of the enemy in our country.

Such proceedings not only degrade the perpetrators and all connected with them, but are subversive of the discipline and efficiency of the army, and destructive of the ends of our present movement.

It must be remembered that we make war only upon armed men, and that we cannot take vengeance for the wrongs that our people have suffered without lowering ourselves in the eyes of all those whose abhorrence has been excited by the atrocities of our enemies, and offending against Him to whom vengeance belongeth, without whose favor, and support our efforts must all prove in vain.

The Commanding General, therefore, earnestly exhorts the troops to abstain with most scrupulous care from unnecessary or wanton injury to private property, and he enjoins upon all officers to arrest and bring to summary punishment all who shall in any way offend against the orders on this subject.

R. E. LEE, General.

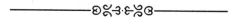

THE MOTHER OF SEVEN SOLDIERS

Mrs. Butler's Response When Introduced as the Sister of Commodore Perry

Charlotte Observer.

Mrs. Butler, the mother of Senator Butler, was a resident of Greenville, S. C. She was quite an interesting character. She reared a large family, and when the war broke out her sons promptly responded to their country's call for volunteers.

As Greenville was but a small town, and there was but one train a day, it was customary for a crowd to assemble at the depot every evening to hear the news from the scene of battle, some gentleman usually reading the paper aloud to the others. And as regularly as the evening came, Mrs. Butler might be on on her way to the station, sitting in her little carriage, or "carry-all," as it was called, driving an old horse which had evidently seen better days. She would take her position, close to the platform, near the reader, and raising her eartrumpet, listen attentively, showing her approval or disapproval as the case might be, by a nod or an emphatic remark.

The following story is told of her: When a division of Sherman's army came through Greenville, their headquarters were on Boyce's lawn, but a short distance from Mrs. Butler's home. Some of the more lawless members of the army scoured the country, pillaging and taking possession of anything on which they could lay their hands. They visited the stable and carried off Mrs. Butler's only horse. Early the following morning she presented herself at headquarters and asked to see the Federal commander. Dr. B—, a Southern gentleman who was present thinking if the general knew her social position, he would feel more inclined to grant her request, introduced her as the "sister of Commodore Perry, our distinguished naval officer." But the patriotic old lady remarked with a good deal of spirit, "I did not come here as the sister of Commodore Perry, but as the mother of seven sons in the Confederate army, and I want my old gray horse."

222 CONFEDERATE WOMEN OF ARKANSAS

It is needless to say that the Federal officer, admiring her independence, promptly restored the animal to its owner.

MISS JULIA ROBERTS, Charlotte, N. C.

---------------⊙⚡3⚡⚡⊙---------------

THE HOMESPUN DRESS

This ballad was written by Miss Carrie Belle Sinclair in the midsummer of 1862.

There was a rivalry with the Augusta girls as to who should have the neatest homespun dress, and from this incident she took the idea and wrote that old war song.

The poem was first published in an Augusta paper and was copied in the Savannah Morning News.

"The Homespun Dress" was sung to the popular air of "The Bonnie Blue Flag," by a member of the "Queen Sisters," an English family, then holding the boards of the theatre, and this, with other songs written by her, soon won for their author the name, "Songbird of the South."

THE HOMESPUN DRESS

Oh yes, I am a Southern girl,
    And glory in the name.
And boast it with far greater pride
    Than glittering wealth or fame.
I envy not the Northern girl
    Her robes of beauty rare,
Though diamonds grace her snowy neck
    And pearls bedeck her hair.

Chorus —

Hurrah! Hurrah!
  For the Sunny South so dear!
Three cheers for the Homespun Dress,
  Our Southern ladies wear!

  My homespun dress is plain, I know,
    My hat's palmetto, too;
  But then it shows what Southern girls
  For Southern rights will do.
  We scorn to wear a bit of silk,
    A bit of Northern lace,
  But make our homespun dress up,
    And wear them with such grace.

Chorus —

  Now Northern goods are out of date;
    And since old Abe's blockade,
  We Southern girls can be content
    With goods that's Southern made,
  We sent the brave from out our land
    To battle with the foe,
  And we will lend a helping hand —
    We love the South you know

Chorus —

  Our land it is a glorious land,
    And ours a glorious cause;
  Then three cheers for the homespun dress,

And for the Southern boys;
We sent our sweethearts to the war,
But, dear girls, never mind,
The soldier never will forget—
The girl he left behind.

Chorus—

A soldier is the lad for me.
A brave heart I adore—
And when the Sunny South is free,
And fighting is no more,
I then will choose a lover brave
From out that glorious band,
The soldier boy that I love best
Shall have my heart and hand.

Chorus—

And now, young men, a word to you,
If you win the fair,
Go to the field where honor calls,
And win your ladies there;
Remember that our brightest smiles
Are for the true and brave,
And that our tears are for the one
That fills a soldier's grave.

Chorus—

—From an Old War Scrapbook

POEM, TO THE WOMEN OF THE CONFEDERACY

Raise the shaft, 'tis for our mothers,
  Set its base with colors fair;
Furl the faded, starry banner
  Round its staff, and leave it there.

Lift it where the earliest sunbeam
  Drives the memory's mist away,
Leave it where the fading twilight
  Lingers longest with the day.

Twine the myrtle with the ivy,
  And the fragrant scented vine;
Bring the white magnolia blossoms
  And the crimson columbine.

North and East and South and Westward,
  From its columns pure and white,
Write upon the peerless marble,
  On its polished tablets, write —

How they toiled and prayed and suffered
  Through the long and bitter years,
Kept the altar fires burning.
  With the increase of their tears;

How their love, in streams of blessing,
  Wore its channels deep and wide,
Bore the fortunes of the battle,
  On its broad and surging tide;

How their faith, that trusted ever,
Rested on the soldier's shield,
Watched above the bloody carnage,
And upon the tented field.

How the summer bloomed and faded,
Yet did Love and Trust abide,
But their hopes, like shattered roses,
With the autumn glory died.

Then from out the burning embers
Love and hope and faith and trust
Soared above the desolation,
Shook their plumage of its dust;

Returning, brought the sprig of olive,
Saw the bow of promise spanned,
And the dawn of peace and plenty
O'er a broad and smiling land.

But the heart knows no forgetting,
And within her silent halls.
Where the fragrant incense rises
And the inner sunlight falls,

Hang the swords and rusty scabbard,
With the coats of faded Gray
And perfumed with myrrh and alloes,
All the flags are laid, away.

And besides the faded banners,

And the urns of storied dust,
Memory stands within the portals,
Keeping watch above her trust.

KATE P. FLENNIKEN
Winnsboro, N. C.

———————————————

LETTER OF MRS. JEFFERSON DAVIS TO J. L. UNDERWOOD

From Underwood's Women of the Confederacy

Hotel Gerard, 123 West Forty-Fourth St.,
New York

October 25, 1905

My Dear Mr. Underwood:

I do not know in all history a finer subject than the heroism of our Southern women, God bless them. I have never forgotten our dear Mrs. Robt. E. Lee, sitting in her arm chair, where she was chained by the most agonizing form of rheumatism, cutting with her dear aching hands soldiers' gloves from waste pieces of their Confederate uniforms furnished to her from the government shops. These she persuaded her girl visitors to sew into gloves for the soldiers. Certainly these scraps were of immense use to all those who could get them, for I do not know how many children's jackets which kept the soldiers' children warm, I had pieced out of the scraps by a poor woman who sat in the basement of the mansion and made them for them.

The ladies picked their old silk pieces into fragments, and spun them into gloves, stockings, and scarfs for the soldiers' necks, etc.; cut up their house linen and scraped it into lint; tore up their sheets and rolled them into bandages; and toasted sweet potatos slices brown, and made substitutes for coffee. They put two tablespoonfuls of sorghum molasses into the water boiled for coffee instead of sugar, and used none other for their little children and families. They covered their old shoes with old kid gloves or with pieces of silk and their little feet looked charming and natty in them. In the country they made their own candles, and one lady sent me three cakes of sweet soap and a small jar of soft soap made from the skin, bones and refuse bits of hams boiled for her family. Another sent me the most exquisite unbleached flax thread, of the smoothest and finest quality, spun by herself. I have never been able to get such thread again. I am still quite feeble, so I must close with the hope that your health will steadily improve and the assurance that I am,

Yours sincerely,
V. JEFFERSON DAVIS

———————————

VIVID HISTORY OF OUR BATTLE FLAG
From the Confederate Veteran, May 1900

Gen. W. L. Cabell, now of Dallas, Texas, who was chief quartermaster of the Confederate army in Virginia at the time referred to, furnished the following to the Veteran May 25, 1900:

When the Confederate army, commanded by Gen. Beauregard, at Manassas and the Federal army confronted each other, it was seen that the Confederate flag (stars and bars) and the stars and stripes at a distance looked so much alike that it was hard to distinguish one from the other. Gen. Beauregard, thinking that serious mistakes might be made in recognizing our troops, after the battle of July 18 at Blackburn Ford, ordered that a small red badge should be worn on the left shoulder by our troops, and, as I was chief quartermaster, ordered me to purchase a large amount of red flannel and to distribute a supply to each regiment. I did so, and a number of regiments placed badges on their left shoulder.

During the battle of Bull Run it was discovered that a great number of Federal soldiers were wearing a similar red badge. I saw those badges on a number of prisoners we captured that day.

Generals Johnston and Beauregard met at Fairfax Courthouse in the latter part of August or early part of September, and determined to have a battle flag for every regiment or detached command that could easily be recognized and easily carried. I was telegraphed to go to them at once at Fairfax Courthouse. Both Gen. Beauregard and Gen. Johnston were in Beauregard's office discussing the kind of flag that should be adopted. Gen. Johnston's design was in the shape of an ellipse, red flag with a blue St. Andrew's cross, white stars on the cross to represent the different Southern States. No white border of any kind was attached to this cross. Gen. Beauregard's design was a rectangle, red with blue St. Andrew's cross and white stars similar to Gen. Johnston's. Both were thoroughly examined by all of us. After we had fully discussed the two styles, taking into consideration the cost of material and the care of making the same, it was decided that the elliptical flag would be harder to make, that it would take more cloth, and that it could not be seen as plain at a distance as the rectangular flag drawn and suggested by Gen. Beauregard, so the latter was adopted. Gen. Johnston yielded promptly to the reasons given by Gen. Beauregard and myself. No one was present but us three. No one knew about this flag but us until an order was issued adopting the "Beauregard Flag," as it was called. He directed me, as chief quartermaster to have the flag made as soon as it could be done.

I immediately issued an address to the good ladies of the South to give me their red and blue silk dresses, and to send them to Captain Collin McRae Selph, quartermaster at Richmond. Va., (Captain Selph lives in New Orleans today), where he was assisted by two elegant young ladies—the two Misses Carey of Baltimore— Mrs. General Henningsen of Savannah, and Mrs. Judge Hopkins of Alabama. The Misses Carey made battle flags for Gens. Beauregard, Van Dorn, and (I think), J. E. Johnston. They made Gen. Beauregard's headquarter flag out of their own silk dresses. It is in Memorial Hall, New Orleans, with a statement of its history by Gen. Beauregard. Gen. Van Dorn's flag was made of heavier material, but was very pretty. Captain Selph had a number of these flags made and sent to me at Manassas, and they were distributed by order of Gen. Beauregard. One flag I had made for the Washington Artillery, and they have it yet. My wife who was in Richmond, made a beautiful flag, out of her own silk dress and sent it to a cousin of hers who commanded an Arkansas regiment. This flag was lost at Elk Horn, but was recaptured by a Missouri Division under Gen. Henry Little. It being impossible to get silk enough to make the great number of flags needed, I had a number made out of the blue and red cotton cloth. I then issued a circular letter to the quartermaster of every regiment and brigade in the army to make the flags, and to use any blue and red cloth suitable that they could get. Gens. Beauregard and Johnston, being good draftsmen, drew their own designs.

The statements going the rounds that this battle flag was first designed by a Federal prisoner is false. There is no truth in it. No living soul except Gens. Beauregard and Johnston and myself knew anything about this flag until the order was issued direct to me to have them made as soon as it could be done.

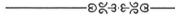

ORIGIN OF UNITED DAUGHTERS
OF THE CONFEDERACY
From the Confederate Veteran, November, 1900

At a regular meeting of Nashville Chapter No. 1, United Daughters of the Confederacy, held in the city of Nashville, Tenn., on November 1, 1900, the following resolution was unanimously adopted:

Whereas, at the Richmond Convention of the United Daughters of the Confederacy in November, 1900, Mrs. J. A. Rounsaville, President of the Georgia Division, suggested that proof should be taken as to who originated the idea of uniting all the organizations of Southern women into one Federation, in order that it might be printed in the minutes of the Montgomery Convention; and whereas, the Nashville Chapter No. 1, United Daughters of Confederacy, have taken proof, and submit the following evidences, substantiating the fact that Mrs. M. C. Goodlett, of Nashville, Tenn., first originated the idea:

On March 25, 1890, the ladies of Nashville organized and had chartered the Ladies' Auxiliary to the Confederate Soldiers' Home, and Mrs. M. C. Goodlett was elected State President thereof.

On May 10, 1892, at a dinner given by the Ladies' Auxiliary, on Summer street, in Nashville, on motion of Mrs. M. C. Goodlett, the name of the Ladies' Auxiliary was changed to Daughters of the Confederacy.

In 1894, Mrs. Goodlett having conceived the idea of organizing all associations of Southern women into one body, to be known as the Daughters of the Confederacy, in May of that year, at a meeting of the Nashville Chapter, the object was brought forward and published in the Nashville American. Shortly thereafter Mrs. Goodlett received a letter from Mrs. L. H. Raines, of Savannah, Ga., indorsing the idea, and requesting that a copy of the constitution, charter, and by-laws of the Nashville Chapter should be sent her for examination, and asking if Savannah women could be organized under the Nashville charter.

Thereafter the Nashville Chapter issued a call, inviting all Southern women to meet with it on September 9th, 1894, in the rooms of Frank Cheatham Bivouac, for the organization of all Daughters of the Confederacy into one federation. The following ladies attended this meeting: Mesdames M. C. Goodlett, John Overton, J. B. Lindsley, William Hume, Isabella Clark, George B. Guild, W. B.Maney, R. H. Dudley, Nathaniel Gooch, W. T. McMurray, A. E. Snyder, John P. Hickman Miss White May, and others, of Nashville; Mrs. L. H. Raines, of Savannah; and Mrs. Myers of Texas. On that night Mrs. Raines went home with Mrs. Goodlett, carrying with her the constitution of the United Confederate Veterans. On the next morning Mrs. Goodlett and Mrs. Raines presented a draft of the new constitution of the new organization to be known as the National Daughters of the Confederacy, which, after being amended, was adopted, and the following officers were elected for the ensuing year: Mrs. M. C. Goodlett, Nashville, President; Mrs. L. H. Raines, Savannah, First Vice-President; Mrs. J. C. Myers, Texas, Second Vice-President; Miss White May, Nashville, Third Vice-President; Mrs. John P. Hickman, Nashville, Secretary; Mrs. J. N. Lindsley, Nashville, Treasurer.

It was also determined at this meeting that the Nashville Chapter should be known as No. 1, and the Savannah Chapter as No. 2. Several errors and inaccuracies being discovered in the constitution as adopted, another meeting was called to meet at the same place on March 30, 1905. This meeting was attended by all the ladies above mentioned, besides several others of the Nashville Chapter, and Mrs. A. T. Smythe, of Charleston, S. C.; Mrs. William Parsley, of Wilmington, N. C.; Mrs. Fleming DuBignon and Miss Lamar, of Savannah, Ga.; and Mrs. R. A. Allison, of Jackson, Tenn.

At this meeting the constitution was amended. Mrs. Katie Cabell Currie was made Vice-President in the place of Mrs. Myers. Mrs. Smythe and Mrs. Parsley were made Vice-Presidents, and the Wilmington Chapter was made No. 3, the Charleston Chapter No. 4, and the Jackson Chapter No. 5.

This proof has been gotten by records in the office of our Secretary of State, proof by the parties who were present at the meetings and from numerous letters from Mrs. L. H. Raines to Mrs. M. C. Goodlett, which are now in the possession of Mrs. Goodlett, and which have been exhibited to and read by the Chapter.

If Mrs. Goodlett did not originate the idea, why was she made the first president, and why was the Nashville Chapter given the honor of being designated as No. 1?

All proof taken, and all letters from Mrs. L. H. Raines, with all original papers, will be submitted to any committee the Convention may see proper to appoint, if it is not convinced by the statements herein set forth. Therefore,

Resolved, by the Nashville Chapter No. 1, that this statement of facts shall be read at the Montgomery Convention of the United Daughters of the Confederacy, and printed in the proceedings of the Convention and in the CONFEDERATE VETERAN.

By order of the Nashville Chapter.

MRS. LIZZIE OVERTON CRAIGHEAD, Pres.

MISS MARTHA A. HILL, Secretary.

ORIGIN OF UNITED SONS OF
CONFEDERATE VETERANS
From the Confederate Veteran, August, 1896

The formation at Richmond the last week of June, 1896, of the Federation to be known as the United Sons of Confederate Veterans should receive the commendation and support of all true Southerners. Its aims, objects and purposes are not to create or foster, in any manner, any feeling against the North, but to hand down to posterity the "story of the glory of the men who wore the gray."

Knowing that "in union there is strength," the sons of those who made the South famous have come together for the systematic and united work of preserving from oblivion the true history of the South. That this step meets with the hearty approval of the "men who wore the gray" is shown by the following resolution, which was adopted at the Convention of the United Confederate Veterans at Richmond, at their regular session:

"Resolved, That this session provide at once for the formation of Sons of Confederate Veterans into a separate national organization. This is urgent from the manifold fact that our ranks are thinning daily, and our loved representatives should step in now and arrange to take charge of Southern history, our relics, mementos and monuments, and stimulate the erection of other monuments to our heroes ere 'taps' are sounded for the last of their fathers."

But before this resolution was adopted the Sons had taken matters in their own hands, and on the evening of

June 30th, 1896, met at the auditorium at Richmond, and arranged for the organization of a Federation themselves. At this meeting a committee was appointed to draft a Constitution for the new Association, but they were unable to prepare the same that evening, and the session adjourned at 11 o'clock to meet the next day.

On July 1st the delegates from the Camp of Sons of Confederate Veterans from the various Southern States, who had been called by the R. E. Lee Camp of Richmond, to assemble for the purpose of forming this Association, adopted a Constitution, similar in every respect to the constitution governing the United Confederate Veterans, and permanently organized the United Sons of Confederate Veterans.

The preamble of this Constitution reads: "To encourage the preservation of history, perpetuate the hallowed memories of brave men, to assist in the observance of Memorial Day, to aid and support all Confederate Veterans, widows and orphans, and to perpetuate the record of the services of every Southern Soldier, these are our common aims. These objects we believe will both promote a purer and better private life, and enhance our desire to maintain the national honor, union and independence of our common country."

The organization of this Association is composed of departments, divisions, brigades and camps.

The Federation has an Executive Head and three Departments, entitled Army of Northern Virginia Department, consisting of the States of North and South Carolina, Maryland, Virginia and Kentucky. The Army of Tennessee Department, consisting of the States of Georgia, Alabama, Tennessee, Mississippi, Louisiana and Florida. The Trans-Mississippi Department, consisting of the States and Territories west of the Mississippi excepting Louisiana. Each State constitutes a division and is commanded by a Major General; the Departments are commanded by a Lieutenant General. The States are furthermore divided into brigades which also have their commanders. In this way the work is thoroughly systematized and is so arranged that the most excellent results can be readily obtained.

The officers elected at this first Convention of the United Sons of Confederate Veterans were as follows: Mr. J. E. B. Stuart, of Richmond, General Commanding; Mr. Robert A. Smyth, of Charleston, Lieutenant General in command of the Department of Northern Virginia; Mr. John L. Hardeman, of Macon, Ga., Lieutenant General in command of the Department of Tennessee. The election of the Lieutenant General of the Trans-Mississippi Department was deferred until the organization of State Divisions in that Department; Mr. R. H. Pinckney, of Charleston, Quartermaster General; Mr. George B. Williamson, of Columbia, Tenn., Inspector General; Dr. Stuart McGuire, of Richmond, Surgeon General; Mr. E. P. McKissick, of Asheville, N. C., Commissary General; Bishop T. F. Gailor, of Tennessee, Grand Chaplain; Mr. T. R. R. Cobb, of Atlanta, Ga., Judge Advocate General.

The officers of this new Association are exerting every effort to thoroughly organize and build up the same, and to this end their efforts will be directed to the formation of camps of Sons in every city and town in the South.

According to the Constitution the Convention of the United Sons of Confederate Veterans is held at the same time and place as the United Confederate Veterans, so that the next convention will meet at Nashville, Tenn.

The General commanding has the power to appoint a staff to aid him in his work, as have also the Lieutenant Generals and the Commanders of Divisions. Gen. J. E. B. Stuart has appointed Mr. Edwin P. Cox, of Richmond, Virginia, his Adjutant General and Chief of Staff. The Lieutenant Generals have not as yet been appointed.

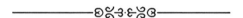

ORIGIN OF UNITED CONFEDERATE VETERANS
By J. M. Lucey

The originator of the idea which culminated in the organization of the United Confederate Veterans is Capt. J. F. Shipp, Commander of the N. B. Forrest Camp, U. C. V., of Chattanooga, Tenn., who was quartermaster general on the staff of General J. B. Gordon, and who now occupies a similar position on the Staff of General Stephen D. Lee. One of his prime objects in advocating and promoting the organization of the United Confederate Veterans was in that way to promote the purchase of the Chickamauga battlefield by the United States government. The movement was started January, 1889. The last session of the Georgia legislature had granted a charter to thirty or forty gentlemen who had been prominent officers in the Confederate armies in the Civil War, many of them being at the time members of the upper and lower houses of the national Congress. The purpose of the Association was to have Congress appropriate a sum of money sufficient to purchase the ground on which the battle of Chickamauga was fought and to make it a grand park. Many influential Northern men who served in the Federal army became interested, as it was intended, by means of Northern and Southern monuments and other marks, to locate the several positions of the armies, so that the men of the Union and Confederate forces might meet often in fraternal reunions, and by relating their experiences "bridge over the bloody chasm." This dream of Capt. Shipp has been more than realized, as there is now a great national military park not only at Chickamauga but also at Shiloh and Vicksburg, and the annual gatherings of Union and Confederate soldiers have been attended with a feeling so fraternal that so far as they are concerned the war is over.

Capt. Shipp purposely selected New Orleans as the place in which to inaugurate the movement for the organization of the United Confederate Veterans, which with the Grand Army of the Republic was to have a general supervision over the parks, recognizing that city as the geographical centre of Confederate sentiment. In New Orleans were already existing three somewhat old associations of Confederate Veterans: The Association of the Army of Northern Virginia, Louisiana Division; The Association of the Army of Tennessee, Louisiana Division; and The Association of the Washington Artillery. In other parts of the South—Arkansas included—there were also Confederate associations some large, others small, but all independent of one another.

It was on the occasion of the annual banquet and reunion of the Louisiana Divison of the Army of Northern Virginia at New Orleans, January 19, 1889, the same being Robert E. Lee's birthday, and approximately Stonewall Jackson's to which Capt. Shipp had been invited, that he sought to advocate and promulgate his plan for the federation of all Confederate Veteran organizations under one constitution and one general commander. There were about 400 prominent Confederate veterans present, chief among whom was Jefferson Davis, whose address, in sympathy in its general tenor with the idea of Capt. Shipp, was on, "The Army of Northern Virginia and Its Leaders." This was his last address, in fact his last appearance in public. His death occurred December 6, 1889. The idea of Capt. Shipp was endorsed at this meeting and upon a call being made by the Louisiana Divisions of the Army of Northern Virginia and of the Army of Tennessee, a convention of the scattered Confederate associations of the South was held in New Orleans, June 10th, 1889, and a plan of organization adopted. The present name was agreed upon and the office of General Commander with staff, was created. Several years later three departments were established: Department of Army of Northern Virginia, Lieutenant General C. Irvine Walker, Commander; Department of Army of Tennessee, Lieutenant General Clement A. Evans, Commander; and the Trans-Mississippi Department, Lieutenant General W. L. Cabell, Commander. Some years afterwards a fourth department, known as the Department of the Northwest, was created. Each of the Southern States was to be commanded by a Major General with brigadiers under him. All these officers from General to Brigadier are elected annually. The above named generals are now in office.

Each state organization meets annually in reunion. Delegates from all the State camps meet in some central Southern city every year in a general reunion and will continue to meet for a few more years, when the mantle of Southern honor will be transferred to the Sons of United Confederate Veterans. The first reunion of the general organization, U. C. V. was held July 3, 4, 5, 1890, at Chattanooga, in compliment to General Shipp. The last one was held in Richmond, Va., May 30, 1907, as a memorial to Jefferson Davis.

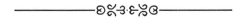

SOUTHERN GIRLS MARRY ONE-LEGGED SOLDIERS

Soon after the war I once expressed my sympathy to a young lady friend who was about to marry a young one-armed soldier. "I want no sympathy. I think it is a great privilege and honor to be the wife of a man who lost his arm fighting for my country," was her prompt reply. That's your Southern girl.

When John Redding, of Randolph County, Ga., was brought home wounded from Chickamauga, it was found necessary to amputate his leg. On the day fixed for the dangerous operation, his many friends were gathered at his father's country home. Among them was Miss Carrie McNeil, to whom he was engaged. After he had passed safely through the ordeal she, of course, was allowed to be the first to go to see him. They were left alone for awhile. The next to go in was an aunt of Miss Carrie's and as she shook hands with poor John and was about to pass on, he said, "Ain't you going to kiss me too?" Ah, what a tale that question told. The gallant soldier had offered to release his betrothed from her engagement, but she said, "no, no, John, I can't give you up, and I love you better than ever," and a kiss had sealed their holy love.

When Tom Phipps, of Randolph County, Ga., came home on crutches he offered to release Miss Maggie Pharham from her engagement. "No, Tom," she said. "We can make a living." There are hundreds of these noble, God-given Carrie McNeils and Maggie Pharhams all over our war wrecked South.

SPECIMEN CASES OF DESERTION
From Underwood's Women of the Confederacy

We by no means excuse or palliate desertion to the enemy, which is universally recognized as one of the basest crimes known to military law; but most of the desertions from the Confederate army occurred during the latter part of the war, and many of them were brought about by the most heart-rendering letters from home, telling of suffering and even starving families, and we cannot class these cases with those who deserted to join the enemy, or to get rid of the hardships and dangers of the army. Some most touching cases came under our observation, but we give only the following incidents as illustrating many other cases.

A distinguished major-general in the Western army has given us this incident. An humble man but very gallant soldier from one of the Gulf States, had enlisted on the assurance of a wealthy planter that he would see his young wife and child should not lack for support.

The brave fellow had served his country faithfully, until one day he received a letter from his wife, saying that the rich neighbor who had promised to keep her from want now utterly refused to give or to sell her anything to eat, unless she would submit to the basest proposals which he was persistently making her, and that unless he could come home she saw nothing but starvation before her and his child. The poor fellow at once applied for a furlough, and was refused. He then went to the gallant soldier who is my informant and stated the case in full, and told him that he must and would go home if he was shot for it the day he returned. The general told him while he could not give him a permit, he did not blame him for his determination.

The next day he was reported "absent without leave," and was hurrying to his home. He moved his wife and child to a place of safety and made provision for their support. Then returning to the neighborhood of his home, he caught the miscreant who had tried to pollute the hearthstone of one who was risking his life for him, dragging him into the woods, tied him to a tree, and administered to him a flogging that he did not soon forget. The brave fellow then hurried back to his regiment, joined his comrades just as they were going into battle, and behaved with such conspicuous gallantry as to make all forget that he had ever, even for a short time, been a "deserter."

The other incident which we shall give was related by General C. A. Battle, in a speech at Tuscumbia, Ala., and is as follows:

During the winter of 1862-3 it was my fortune to be president of one of the courts-martial of the Army of Northern Virginia. One bleak December morning, while the snow covered the ground and the winds howled around our camp, I left my bivouac fire to attend the session of the court. Winding for miles along uncertain paths, I at length arrived at the court-ground at Round Oak Church. Day after day it had been our duty to try the gallant soldiers of that army charged with violations of military law; but never had I on any previous occasion been greeted by such anxious spectators as on that morning awaited the opening of the court. Case after case was disposed of, and at length the case of "The Confederate States vs. Edward Cooper" was called; charge, desertion. A low murmur rose spontaneously from the battle-scarred spectators as a young artillery man rose from the prisoner's bench, and, in response to the question, "Guilty or not guilty?" answered, "Not guilty."

The judge advocate was proceeding to open the prosecution, when the court, observing that the prisoner was unattended by counsel, interposed and inquired of the accused, "Who is your counsel?"

He replied, "I have no counsel."

Supposing that it was his purpose to represent himself before the court, the judge advocate was instructed to proceed. Every charge and specification against the prisoner was sustained.

The prisoner was then told to introduce his witnesses.

He replied, "I have no witnesses."

Astonished at the calmness with which he seemed to be submitting to what he regarded as inevitable fate, I said to him, "Have you no defense? Is it possible that you abandoned your comrades and deserted your colors in the presence of the enemy without any reason?"

He replied, "There was a reason, but it will not avail me before a military court."

I said, "Perhaps you are mistaken; you are charged with the highest crime known to military law, and it is your duty to make known the causes that influenced your actions."

For the first time his manly form trembled and his blue eyes swam in tears. Approaching the president of the court, he presented a letter, saying as he did so, "There, colonel, is what did it." I opened the letter, and in a moment my eyes filled with tears.

It was passed from one to another of the court until all had seen it, and those stern warriors who had passed with Stonewall Jackson through a hundred battles wept like little children. Soon as I sufficiently recovered my self-possession, I read the letter as the prisoner's defense. It was in these words:

My Dear Edward: I have always been proud of you, and since your connection with the Confederate army I have been prouder of you than ever before. I would not have you do anything wrong for the world; but before God, Edward, unless you come home we must die. Last night I was aroused by little Eddie's crying. I called and said, "What's the matter, Eddie?" and he said, "Oh, mamma, I'm so hungry." And Lucy, Edward, your darling Lucy, she never complains, but, she is growing thinner and thinner every day. And before God, Edward, unless you come home we must die.

Your Mary.

Turning to the prisoner, I asked, "What did you do when you received this letter?"

He replied, "I made application for a furlough, and it was rejected; again I made application, and it was rejected; and that night, as I wandered backward and forward in the camp, thinking of my home, with the mild eyes of Lucy looking up to me, and the burning words of Mary sinking in my brain, I was no longer the Confederate soldier, but I was the father of Lucy and the husband of Mary, and I would have passed those lines if every gun in the battery had fired upon me. I went to my home. Mary ran out to meet me, her angel arms embraced me, and she whispered, 'O, Edward, I am so happy. I am so glad you got your furlough.' She must have felt me shudder, for she turned pale as death, and, catching her breath at every word, she said, 'Have you come without your furlough? O, Edward, Edward'. go back, go back. Let me and my children go down together to the grave, but O, for heaven's sake, save the honor of our name. And here I am, gentlemen, not brought here by military power, but in obedience to the command of Mary to abide the sentence of your court."

Every officer of that court-martial felt the force of the prisoner's words. Before them stood, in beatific vision, the eloquent pleader for the husband's and father's wrongs; but they had been trained by their great leader, Robert E. Lee, to tread the path of duty though the lightning's flash scorched the ground beneath their feet, and each in his turn pronounced the verdict: "Guilty." Fortunately for humanity, fortunately for the Confederacy, the proceedings of the court were reviewed by the commanding-general, and upon the record was written:

Headquarters Army of Northern Virginia.

The finding of the court is approved. The prisoner is pardoned and will report to his company.

R. E. Lee, General.

During the subsequent battle, when shot and shell were falling "like torrents from the mountain cloud," my attention was directed to the fact that one of our batteries was being silenced by the concentrated fire of the enemy. When I reached the battery every gun but one had been dismantled, and by it stood a solitary soldier, with the blood streaming from his side. As he recognized me, he elevated his voice above the roar of battle, and said, "General, I have one shell left. Tell me, have I saved the honor of Mary and Lucy?" I raised my hat. Once more a Confederate shell went crashing through the ranks of the enemy, and the hero sank by his gun to rise no more.

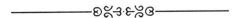

WOMAN'S DEVOTION
General D. H. Maury, in Southern Historical Papers

The history of Winchester is replete with romantic and glorious memories of the late war. One of the most interesting of these has been perpetuated by the glowing pencil of Oregon Wilson, himself a native of this valley, and the fine picture he has made of the incident portrayed by him has drawn tears from many who loved their Southern country and the devoted women who elevated and sanctified by their heroic sacrifice the cause which, borne down for a time, now rises again to honor all who sustained it.

That truth, which is stranger than fiction, is stronger, too. The simple historic facts which gave Wilson the theme of his great pictures, a cut of which appears on another page of this book, gains nothing from the romantic glamour his beautiful art has thrown about the actors in the story.

In 1864, General Ramseur, commanding a Confederate force near Winchester, was suddenly attacked by a Federal force under General Averell, and after a sharp encounter was forced back through the town. The battlefield was near the residence of Mr. Rutherford, about two miles distant, and the wounded were gathered in his house and yard. The Confederate surgeons left in charge of the wounded men appealed to the women of Winchester (the men had all gone off to the war) to come out and aid in dressing the wounds and nursing the wounded. As was always the way of these Winchester women, they promptly responded to this appeal, and on the —day of July, more than twenty ladies went out to Mr. Rutherford's to minister to their suffering countrymen. There were more than sixty severely wounded men who had been collected from the battlefield and were lying in the house and garden of Mr. Rutherford. The weather was warm, and those out of doors were as comfortable and as quiet as those within. Amongst them was a beardless boy named Randolph Ridgely; he was severely hurt; his thigh was broken by a bullet and his sufferings were very great; his nervous system was shocked and unstrung, and he could find no rest. The kind surgeon in charge of him had many others to care for; he felt that quiet sleep was all important for his young patient, and he placed him in the charge of a young girl who had accompanied these ladies from Winchester; told her his life depended on his having quiet sleep that night; showed her how best to support his head, and promised to return to see after his condition as soon and as often his duties to the other wounded would permit.

All through that anxious night the brave girl sat, sustaining the head of the wounded youth and carefully guarding him against everything that could disturb his rest or break the slumber into which he gently sank, and which was to save his life. She only knew and felt that a brave Confederate life depended on her care. She had never seen him before, nor has she ever seen him since. And when at dawn the surgeon came to her, he found her still watching and faithful, just as he had left her at dark—as only a true woman, as we love to believe our Virginia women, can be. The soldier had slept soundly. He awoke only once during the night, when tired nature forced his nurse to change her posture; and when after the morning came she was relieved of her charge, and she felt ill of the exhaustion and exposure of that night, her consolation during the weary weeks she lay suffering was that she had saved a brave soldier for her country.

In the succeeding year, Captain Hancock, of the Louisiana Infantry, was brought to Winchester, wounded and a prisoner. He lay many weeks in the hospital, and when nearly recovered of his wounds, was notified that he would be sent to Fort Delaware. As the time drew near for his consignment to this hopeless prison he confided to Miss Lenie Russell, the same young girl who had saved young Ridgely's life, that he was engaged to be married to a young lady of lower Virginia, and was resolved to make his escape. She cordially entered into his plans, and aided in their successful accomplishment. The citizens of Winchester were permitted sometimes to send articles of food and comfort to the sick and wounded Confederates, and Miss Russell availed herself of this to procure the escape of the gallant captain. She caused him to don the badge of a hospital attendant, take a market basket on his arm and accompany her to a house, whence he might, with least danger of detection and arrest, effect his return to his own lines. Captain Hanock made good use of his opportunity and safely rejoined his comrades; survived the war; married his sweetheart, and to this day omits no occasion for showing his respect and gratitude for the generous woman to whose courage and address he owes his freedom and his happiness.

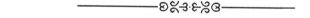

THE CONFEDERATE MUSEUM OF RICHMOND
From Underwood's Women of the Confederacy

This house, built for a gentleman's private residence, was thus occupied until 1862, when Mr. Lewis Crenshaw, the owner, sold it to the city of Richmond for the use of the Confederate government. The city having furnished it, offered it to Mr. Davis, but he refused to accept the gift. The Confederate governnment then rented it for the "Executive Mansion" of the Confederate States. President Davis lived here with his family, using the house both in a private and official capacity.

The present "Mississippi" room was his study, where he often held important conferences with his great leaders. In this house amid the cares of state, joy and sorrow, "Winnie" the cherished daughter, was born, and here "Little Joe," died from the effects of a fall from the back porch. It remained Mr. Davis's home until the evacuation of the city of Richmond. He left with the government officials on the night of April 2, 1865. On the morning of April 3, 1865, General Godfrey Witzel, in command of the Federal troops, upon entering the city, made this house his headquarters. It was thus occupied by the United States Government during the five years Virginia was under military rule, and called "District No. 1."

In the present "Georgia" room, a day or two after the evacuation, Mr. Lincoln was received. He was in the city only a few hours. When at last the military was removed and the house vacated, the city at once took possession, using it as a public school for more than twenty years. In order to make it more comfortable for school purposes, a few unimportant alterations were made. It was the first public school in the city. War had left its impress on the building, and the constant tread of little feet did almost as much damage. It was with great distress that our people (particularly the women), saw the "White House of the Confederacy" put to such uses, and rapidly falling into decay. To save it from destruction, a mass-meeting was called to take steps for its restoration. A society was formed, called the "Confederate Memorial Literary Society," whose aim was the preservation of the mansion. Their first act was to petition the city to place it in their hands, to be used as a memorial to President Davis and a museum of those never-to-be-forgotten days, '61-'65. It was amazing to see the wide-spread enthusiasm aroused by the plan. With as little delay as possible the city, acting through aldermen and council made the deed of conveyance, which was ratified by the then Mayor of Richmond, the Hon. J. Taylor Ellyson.

The dilapidation of the entire property was extreme, but to its restoration and preservation the society had pledged itself. They had no money—the city had already given its part—what could be done? To raise the needed funds it was decided to hold a "memorial bazaar" in Richmond for the joint benefit of the museum and the monument to the private soldier and sailor.

All through the South the plan of the museum and the bazaar was heartily endorsed; so that donations of every kind poured in. Each State of the Confederacy was represented by a booth, with the name, shield, and the flag of her State. The whole sum realized was $31,400. Half of this was given to complete the monument to the private soldiers and sailors now standing on Libby Hill, and the other half went to the museum.

The partition walls were already of brick, and the whole house had been strongly and well built, but the entire building was now made fireproof, and every other possible precaution taken for its safety. In every particular the old house in its entirety was preserved, the wood work (replaced by iron) being used for souvenirs. The repairs were so extensive that the building was not ready for occupancy until late in 1895.

On February 22, 1896, the dedication service was held, and the museum formally throw open to the public.

But the house was entirely empty. Rapidly the memorials were gathered from each loyal State and placed in their several rooms. From start to finish the whole work has been a free-will offering to the beloved cause.

The treasury had been nearly exhausted by the restoration of the building. The current expenes were met only by the strictest economy, and largely carried on by faith. In the past nine years much has been accomplished. The institution is free from debt; and the museum is now widely known. But much lies ahead in the ideal the patriotic women have set before them and the work grows larger, more important and far reaching as it is approached. Such is the interest felt in the museum that during the past year they have had 7,459 visitors, of whom 3,717 were from the North. It is by these door fees that the expenses are met.

It would be quite impossible to enumerate all the articles of interest to be found here. The memorials gathered are not only interesting in themselves, but invaluable for the truth and lessons which they teach. Historians in search of information can here obtain original data in regard to the "War between the States." The United States government has already made use of these records for its new Navy Register. Each Confederate State is hereby represented by a room, set apart in special honor of her sons and their deeds. A regent in that State has it in charge, and is responsible for its contents and appearance. A vice-regent (as far as possible a native of that State, but residing in Richmond) gives her personal supervision to the room and its needs. The labor is incessant, and would be impossible, but for the fact that it is impelled by a sense of sacred love and duty.

Of the women of the Confederacy, of our brave and uncomplaining soldier, of their great leaders, as well as of our illustrious chief, it well may be said:

"Would you see their monument?
Look around."

———————————————

BARBARA FRIETCHIE

Here is a part of the story of the Maryland woman and the Federal flag in the famous poem of John G. Whittier:

"Bravest of all in Fredericktown
She took up the flag the men hauled down;
In her attic window the staff she set
To show that one heart was loyal yet.
Up the street came the rebel tread,
Stonewall Jackson riding ahead;
Under his slouch hat left and right
He glanced; the old flag met his sight.
"Halt," the dust-brown ranks stood fast,
"Fire," out blazed the rifle blast,
It shivered the window pane and sash,
It rent the banner with seam and gash,
Quick as it fell from the broken staff,
Dame Barbara snatched the silken scarf."

This is poetry, but it is not history. It is not truth. It does not sound like it. Nobody but men like Whittier, blinded by New England prejudice and steeped in ignorance of Southern people, would for a moment have thought Stonewall Jackson capable of giving an order to fire on a woman. None of the story sounds at all like "Stonewall Jackson." To their credit the later editions of Whittier's poems cast a grave doubt on the truth of the story, and now Mr. John McLean, an old next door neighbor to the genuine Barbara Frietchie, has given to Mr. Smith Clayton, of the Atlanta Journal, the true story showing Whittier's tale to be nothing but a myth. Mr. Clayton says:

"Coming up to Washington from Richmond the other day, I brushed up an acquaintance with a very pleasant, intelligent and, by the way, handsome gentleman, Mr. John McLean, a conductor on the Richmond, Frederickburg and Washington Railroad. In the course of conversation he mentioned Frederick, Md. I laughed and said:

"Did you ever meet Barbara Frietchie?"

"Why, my dear sir," he replied, "She lived just across the street from my father's home."

"You don't say so?"

"It's a fact; and let me tell you that poem is a 'fake' pure and simple. I was a child during the war, but I'll give you the truth about Barbara Frietchie as I got it from the lips of my father and mother."

And then he told me this interesting story:

"Ever been to Frederick?"

"No."

"Well just where the turn pike enters the town my father and mother lived in the old homestead. Directly across the way lived Mr. Frietchie. He was a tailor, and a good, clever man and honest citizen. His house had two stories. On the ground, or street floor, was his shop. The family lived up stairs. There was a balcony to the upper story of the house facing the street. It was from that balcony that the flag was waved, but Barbara Frietchie had no more to do with it than you. General Stonewall Jackson, returning from Monocacy passed through Frederick at the head of his army. He entered the town by the turn pike and marched between the house of Mr. Frietchie and the home of my parents. There was a United States flag in the tailor's house. His eldest daughter, Mary Quantrell, thinking that the Union army was coming, mistaking Jackson's men for the Federals seized this flag, ran out upon the balcony and waved it. Observing her, General Stonewall Jackson, who was riding at the head of his troops, took off his hat and ordered his men to uncover their heads. They did so, and General Jackson said that he gave the order to uncover because he wanted his men to show proper appreciation of a woman who had the loyalty and patriotism to stand up for her side. Those are the facts. My parents were there. They told me. I tell you. There was no sticking a flag staff in any window. No order by General Jackson to 'Halt' and 'Fire;' no seizing of the flag and waving it after it had been shot from the staff; no begging General Jackson to shoot anybody's grey head, but to 'spare the flag of his country'— all of this is described in the poem—but none of it happened. Very funny about Barbara Frietchie being four score and ten."

"Who was Barbara Frietchie?"

"Why, she was the young daughter of Mr. Frietchie—the young sister of Mary Quantrell, who waved the flag—that's all."

Mr. McLean told me that he had three brothers in the Federal army. His brother was doorkeeper of the Maryland Assembly and his uncle a member during the stormy sessions held at Frederick, when that body hotly discussed, for many days, the question as to whether Maryland should secede.

―――――――◦◦◦―――――――

THE CONQUERED BANNER
By Father Abram Ryan

Furl that banner! for 'tis weary,
Round its staff 'tis drooping dreary;
    Furl it, fold it, it is best;
For there's not a man to wave it
For there's not a sword to save it,
For there's not one left to lave it
In the blood which heroes gave it,
And its foes now scorn and brave it;
    Furl it, bide it, let rest.

Take that banner down! 'tis tattered,
Broken is its staff and shattered,
And the valiant hosts are scattered,
    Over whom it floated high,
Oh, 'tis hard for us to fold it,
Hard to think there's none to hold it,
Hard that those who once unrolled it,

Now must furl it with a sigh.

Furl that banner, furl it sadly—
Once ten thousand hailed it gladly,
And ten thousand wildly, madly,
    Swore it should forever wave;
Swore that foeman's sword could never
Hearts like theirs entwined dissever,
Till that flag would float forever
    O'er their freedom or their grave.

Furl it, for the hands that grasped it,
And the hearts that fondly clasped it,
    Cold and dead are lying low;
For, though conquered, they adore it,
Love the cold, dead hands that bore it,
Weep for those who fell before it,
Pardon those who trailed and tore it,
And oh! how wildly they deplore it—
    Now to furl and fold it so.

Furl that banner! true 'tis gory,
Yet 'tis wreathed around with glory,
And 'twill live in song and story,
    Though its folds are in the dust;
For its fame on brightest pages,
Penned by poets and by sages,
Shall go sounding down the ages,
    Furl its folds though now we must.

Furl that banner! softly, slowly;
Treat it gently,—it is holy—
    For it droops above the dead;

> Touch it not, unfold it never,
> Let it droop there, furled forever,
> For its people's hopes are dead.

Perhaps no poem ever touched and thrilled the hearts of the people of the South as has the "Conquered Banner" by Father Ryan. It came from the heart of the poet at a time when the Southland stood in grief and in untold sorrow. Though his face wore a serious and almost sad aspect, he dearly loved little children and would frequently gather them about him and interest them with some tale. One Christmas, a little girl presented him with a pretty little scroll of the "Conquered Banner." His lips quivered and, placing his hand upon the head of the child as he gave his blessing in gratitude for the gift, he said to her, call your little sisters and I will tell a story.

"Many people said that the 'Conquered Banner' was a great poem. I did not think so when I wrote it, but a poor woman who did not have much education, but whose heart was filled with love for the South thought so and if it had not been for her this poem would have been swept out of the house and burned up and I would never have had this pretty book mark or this true story to tell you.

"I was at Knoxville when the news came that General Lee had surrenedered at Appomatox court house. It was night and I was sitting in my room in a house where many of the regiments of which I was Chaplain were quartered, when an old comrade came in and said to me: 'All is lost, General Lee has surrendered.' I looked at him, I knew by his whitened face that the news was too true, I bowed my head upon the table and wept long and bitterly. Then a thousand thoughts came rushing through my brain. I could not control them. That banner was conquered, its folds must be furled but its story had to be told. We were very poor my dear children in the days of the war. I looked around for a piece of paper to give expression to the thoughts that cried out within me. All that I could find was a piece of brown wrapping paper that layed on the table about an old pair of shoes that a friend had sent me. I seized this piece of paper and wrote the 'Conquered Banner.' Then I went to bed. The next morning the regiment was ordered away and I thought no more of the lines written in such sorrow and desolation of spirit on that fearful night. What was my astonishment a few weeks later to see them appear above my name in a Louisville paper. The poor woman who kept the house in Knoxville had gone as she afterwards told me, into the room where I had slept and was about to throw the piece of paper into the fire when she saw that there was something written upon it. She said that she sat down and cried and copying them she sent the lines to a newspaper in Louisville. And that is how the 'Conquered Banner' got into print. That is the story of this pretty little scroll you have painted for me."

The writer may add that a monument to the memory of Father Ryan will be erected very soon in his home — Mobile, Ala.

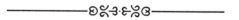

INDEX